Table of Contents

Essential Italy

MOZZARELLA IN CARROZZA

2 eggs
⅓ cup milk
¼ teaspoon salt
⅛ teaspoon black pepper
8 slices country Italian bread
6 ounces fresh mozzarella, cut into ¼-inch slices
8 oil-packed sun-dried tomatoes, drained and cut into strips
8 to 12 fresh basil leaves, torn
1½ tablespoons olive oil

1. Whisk eggs, milk, salt and pepper in shallow bowl or baking dish until well blended.

2. Place four bread slices on work surface. Top with mozzarella, sun-dried tomatoes, basil and remaining bread slices.

3. Heat oil in large skillet over medium heat. Dip sandwiches in egg mixture, turning and pressing to coat completely. Add sandwiches to skillet; cook about 5 minutes per side or until golden brown. Cut into strips or squares.

Makes about 8 appetizer servings

Tip: To serve these sandwiches as a snack or lunch instead of an appetizer, cut them in half instead of squares.

ANTIPASTI

ANTIPASTI

FRIED CALAMARI WITH TARTAR SAUCE

- **Tartar Sauce (recipe follows)**
- **1 pound cleaned squid (body tubes, tentacles or a combination), rinsed and patted dry**
- **¾ cup plain dry bread crumbs**
- **1 egg**
- **1 tablespoon milk**
- **Vegetable oil**
- **Lemon wedges (optional)**

1. Prepare Tartar Sauce. Line baking sheet with waxed paper. Cut squid into ¼-inch rings.

2. Place bread crumbs in medium bowl. Beat egg and milk in separate medium bowl. Add squid; stir to coat well. Transfer squid to bread crumbs; toss to coat. Place on prepared baking sheet. Refrigerate 15 minutes.

3. Heat 1½ inches oil in large heavy saucepan to 350°F; adjust heat to maintain temperature of oil.* Fry squid in batches, 8 to 10 pieces at a time, 45 seconds or until golden brown. (Squid will pop and spatter during frying; do not stand too close to saucepan.) *Do not overcook squid or it will become tough.* Remove with slotted spoon; drain on paper towels.

4. Serve immediately with Tartar Sauce and lemon wedges, if desired.

Makes 2 to 3 servings

**To shallow fry squid, heat about ¼ inch oil in large skillet over medium-high heat; reduce heat to medium. Add single layer of squid to oil without crowding. Cook 1 minute per side or until golden brown. Drain on paper towels.*

TARTAR SAUCE

- **1⅓ cups mayonnaise**
- **2 tablespoons chopped fresh Italian parsley**
- **1 green onion, thinly sliced**
- **1 tablespoon drained capers, minced**
- **1 small sweet gherkin or pickle, minced**

Combine all ingredients in small bowl; mix well. Cover and refrigerate until ready to serve.

Makes about 1⅓ cups

MEDITERRANEAN FRITTATA

- **¼ cup extra virgin olive oil**
- **1 cup thinly sliced onions**
- **1 can (about 14 ounces) whole peeled tomatoes, drained and chopped**
- **¼ pound prosciutto or cooked ham, chopped**
- **¼ cup grated Parmesan cheese**
- **2 tablespoons chopped fresh parsley**
- **½ teaspoon dried marjoram**
- **¼ teaspoon salt**
- **¼ teaspoon dried basil**
- **Generous dash black pepper**
- **6 eggs**
- **2 tablespoons butter**

1. Heat oil in large skillet over medium-high heat. Add onions; cook and stir 6 to 8 minutes until soft and golden. Reduce heat to medium. Add tomatoes; cook 5 minutes. Remove tomatoes and onions to large bowl with slotted spoon; discard drippings. Cool tomato mixture to room temperature.

2. Stir prosciutto, Parmesan, parsley, marjoram, salt, basil and pepper into tomato mixture. Whisk eggs in small bowl; stir into prosciutto mixture.

3. Preheat broiler. Heat butter in medium broilerproof skillet over medium heat until melted and bubbly; reduce heat to low. Add egg mixture to skillet, spreading evenly. Cook 8 to 10 minutes until all but top ¼ inch of frittata is set; shake pan gently to test. *Do not stir.*

4. Place pan under broiler about 4 inches from heat. Broil 1 to 2 minutes until top of frittata is set. (Do not brown or frittata will be dry.) Serve hot or at room temperature. Cut into wedges. *Makes 6 to 8 appetizer servings*

EGGPLANT ROLLS

1 large eggplant (about 1¼ pounds)
3 tablespoons extra virgin olive oil
Salt and black pepper
1 cup ricotta cheese
½ cup grated Asiago cheese
¼ cup julienned or chopped oil-packed sun-dried tomatoes
¼ cup chopped fresh basil or Italian parsley
⅛ teaspoon red pepper flakes
Cherry tomatoes, halved (optional)
Fresh thyme (optional)

1. Preheat broiler. Trim stem end from eggplant; discard. Peel eggplant, if desired. Cut eggplant lengthwise into 6 slices about ¼ inch thick. Brush both sides of eggplant slices with oil; sprinkle with salt and pepper. Place on rack of broiler pan.

2. Broil 4 inches from heat 4 to 5 minutes per side or until golden brown and slightly softened. Let cool to room temperature.

3. Combine ricotta, Asiago, sun-dried tomatoes, basil and red pepper flakes in small bowl; mix well. Spread mixture evenly over eggplant slices. Roll up and cut each roll in half crosswise. Arrange rolls, seam side down, on serving platter. Garnish with cherry tomatoes and thyme. Serve warm or at room temperature.

Makes 6 appetizer servings

CLASSIC TOMATO BRUSCHETTA

- **1 tablespoon olive oil**
- **1 small clove garlic, minced**
- **2 cups chopped seeded tomatoes (3 medium)**
- **⅛ teaspoon salt**
- **Black pepper**
- **Italian bread slices**

1. Preheat oven to 350°F. Heat oil and garlic in small skillet over medium heat 2 minutes, stirring occasionally. Remove from heat. Stir in tomatoes, salt and pepper; mix well.

2. Place bread slices on baking sheet. Bake 8 to 10 minutes or until golden brown. Cool slightly. Top with tomato mixture. *Makes 4 servings*

Variations: Add 2 tablespoons slivered fresh basil to the tomato mixture in step 1 or sprinkle the basil on top. Top the bruschetta with shaved Asiago or Parmesan cheese.

PEPERONATA

- **1 tablespoon extra virgin olive oil**
- **4 large red, yellow and/or orange bell peppers, cut into thin strips**
- **2 cloves garlic, coarsely chopped**
- **12 pimiento-stuffed green olives or pitted black olives, cut into halves**
- **2 to 3 tablespoons white or red wine vinegar**
- **¼ teaspoon salt**
- **¼ teaspoon black pepper**

1. Heat oil in large skillet over medium-high heat. Add bell peppers; cook 8 to 9 minutes or until edges begin to brown, stirring frequently.

2. Reduce heat to medium. Add garlic; cook and stir 1 to 2 minutes. *Do not allow garlic to brown.* Add olives, vinegar, salt and black pepper; cook 1 to 2 minutes or until all liquid has evaporated. *Makes 4 to 5 servings*

Note: Peperonata is a very versatile dish. It can be served hot as a condiment or as a side dish with meat dishes. It can also be chilled and served as part of an antipasti selection.

PARMESAN POLENTA

4 cups vegetable or chicken broth
1 small onion, minced
4 cloves garlic, minced
1 tablespoon minced fresh rosemary *or* 1 teaspoon dried rosemary
½ teaspoon salt
1¼ cups yellow cornmeal
6 tablespoons grated Parmesan cheese
1 tablespoon olive oil, divided

1. Spray 11×7-inch baking pan with nonstick cooking spray. Spray one side of 7-inch sheet of waxed paper with cooking spray.

2. Combine broth, onion, garlic, rosemary and salt in medium saucepan; bring to a boil over high heat. Add cornmeal gradually, stirring constantly. Reduce heat to medium; simmer 30 minutes or until mixture is consistency of thick mashed potatoes. Remove from heat; stir in Parmesan.

3. Spread polenta evenly in prepared pan; place waxed paper, sprayed side down, on polenta and smooth surface. (If surface is bumpy, it is more likely to stick to grill.) Cool on wire rack 15 minutes or until firm. Remove waxed paper; cut into 6 squares and remove from pan.

4. Spray grid with cooking spray. Preheat grill. Brush tops of squares with half of oil.

5. Grill polenta, oil side down, on covered grill over low to medium heat 6 to 8 minutes or until golden. Brush with remaining oil; turn and grill 6 to 8 minutes or until golden. Serve warm.

Makes 6 servings

MARINATED ANTIPASTO

¼ cup extra virgin olive oil
2 tablespoons balsamic vinegar
1 clove garlic, minced
½ teaspoon sugar
½ teaspoon salt
¼ teaspoon black pepper
1 pint (2 cups) cherry tomatoes
1 can (about 14 ounces) quartered artichoke hearts, drained
8 ounces small balls or cubes of fresh mozzarella cheese
1 cup drained pitted kalamata olives
¼ cup sliced fresh basil
Lettuce leaves

1. Whisk oil, vinegar, garlic, sugar, salt and pepper in medium bowl. Add tomatoes, artichokes, mozzarella, olives and basil; toss to coat. Let stand at room temperature 30 minutes.

2. Line platter with lettuce. Arrange antipasto over lettuce; serve at room temperature.

Makes about 5 cups (12 appetizer servings)

Tip You can serve the antipasto with toothpicks as an appetizer, or spoon it over Bibb lettuce leaves for a first-course salad.

ROASTED PEPPER & OLIVE FOCACCIA

1 package (¼ ounce) active dry yeast
1 teaspoon sugar
1½ cups warm water (105° to 110°F)
4 cups all-purpose flour, divided
7 tablespoons olive oil, divided
1 teaspoon salt
¼ cup bottled roasted red peppers, drained and cut into strips
¼ cup pitted black olives

1. Sprinkle yeast and sugar over warm water in large bowl; stir until dissolved. Let stand 5 minutes or until mixture is bubbly. Add 3½ cups flour, 3 tablespoons oil and salt, stirring until soft dough forms.

2. Turn out dough onto lightly floured surface. Knead 5 minutes or until smooth and elastic, gradually adding remaining flour to prevent sticking, if necessary. Shape dough into ball; place in large lightly greased bowl. Turn dough over to grease top. Cover; let rise in warm place 1 hour or until doubled.

3. Brush 15×10-inch jelly-roll pan with 1 tablespoon oil. Punch down dough. Turn out dough onto lightly floured surface. Flatten into rectangle; roll out almost to size of pan. Place dough in pan; gently press dough to edges. Poke surface of dough with end of wooden spoon handle, making indentations every 1 or 2 inches. Brush with remaining 3 tablespoons oil. Gently press peppers and olives into dough. Cover; let rise in warm place 30 minutes or until doubled.

4. Preheat oven to 450°F. Bake 12 to 18 minutes or until golden brown. Cut into squares or rectangles. Serve warm. *Makes 12 servings*

ARANCINI

Risotto alla Milanese (recipe follows)
1½ cups Italian seasoned dry bread crumbs
3 egg whites
12 (½-inch) pieces fresh mozzarella cheese
12 (½-inch) pieces Parmigiano-Reggiano cheese
12 (¼-inch) cubes ham
2 cups canola oil

1. Prepare Risotto alla Milanese. Spread on nonstick baking sheet; cool completely. Spread bread crumbs on plate. Beat egg whites in small bowl.

2. Line baking sheet with waxed paper. Working with 2 tablespoons risotto at a time, flatten into 3-inch disc. Place one piece each of mozzarella, Parmigiano-Reggiano and ham in center of disc. Fold edges up to cover filling, gently pinching seams to seal. Roll between palms to form egg-size ball.

3. Dip in bread crumbs, then egg whites, then again in bread crumbs. Place on prepared baking sheet. Repeat with remaining ingredients. Cover and refrigerate 1 hour or overnight.

4. Heat oil in large deep skillet to 360°F. Cook 1 minute per side or until golden brown. Transfer to wire rack. Serve warm. *Makes 12 small arancini*

RISOTTO ALLA MILANESE

4 cups chicken or vegetable broth
2 tablespoons butter
2 tablespoons olive oil
1 shallot, minced
1 cup arborio rice
¼ cup white wine
1 generous pinch saffron threads, ground to a powder
¼ cup grated Parmesan cheese
Salt and black pepper

continued on page 20

Arancini, continued

1. Bring broth to a simmer in medium saucepan over medium-heat heat; keep warm over low heat.

2. Heat butter and oil in deep saucepan over medium-high heat. Add shallot; cook and stir 30 seconds or just until beginning to brown.

3. Add rice; cook and stir 1 to 2 minutes or until edges of rice become translucent. Add wine and saffron; cook and stir until wine evaporates.

4. Reduce heat to medium-low. Add ½ cup broth, stirring constantly until broth is absorbed. Repeat until all broth is used. Stir in Parmesan. Season with salt and pepper. *Makes 4 servings*

BAGNA CAUDA

¾ cup olive oil
6 tablespoons butter, softened
12 anchovy fillets, drained
6 cloves garlic, peeled
⅛ teaspoon red pepper flakes
Assorted foods for dipping: endive spears, cauliflower florets, cucumber spears, carrot sticks, zucchini spears, red bell pepper strips, sugar snap peas or Italian bread slices

Slow Cooker Directions

1. Combine oil, butter, anchovies, garlic and red pepper flakes in food processor; process until smooth. Transfer to small slow cooker.

2. Cover; cook on LOW 2 hours or on HIGH 1 hour or until mixture is heated through. Turn slow cooker to LOW or WARM; serve with assorted dippers. *Makes 10 to 12 servings*

Note: Bagna cauda is a warm Italian dip similar to fondue. The name means "warm bath" in Italian.

Savory Bites

MOZZARELLA & PROSCIUTTO BITES

16 to 20 small bamboo skewers or toothpicks
8 ounces fresh mozzarella
¼ cup chopped fresh basil
½ teaspoon black pepper
6 to 8 thin slices prosciutto

1. Soak skewers in water 20 minutes to prevent burning. Cut mozzarella into 1- to 1½-inch chunks.* Place on paper towel-lined plate; sprinkle with basil and pepper, turning to coat all sides.

2. Cut prosciutto slices crosswise into thirds. Tightly wrap one prosciutto slice around each mozzarella piece, covering completely. Insert skewer into each piece. Freeze skewers 15 minutes to firm.

3. Preheat broiler. Line broiler pan or baking sheet with foil. Place skewers on prepared pan; broil about 3 minutes or until prosciutto begins to crisp, turning once. Serve immediately. *Makes 16 to 20 pieces*

**You can also substitute one 8-ounce container of small fresh mozzarella balls (ciliegine). One 8-ounce container contains 24 balls.*

FAST PESTO FOCACCIA

- **1 package (about 14 ounces) refrigerated pizza dough**
- **2 tablespoons pesto sauce**
- **4 oil-packed sun-dried tomatoes, drained and chopped**

1. Preheat oven to 425°F. Lightly grease 8-inch square baking pan. Unroll pizza dough. Fold in half; press gently into pan.

2. Spread pesto evenly over dough. Sprinkle tomatoes over pesto and press into dough. Make indentations in dough every 2 inches with handle of wooden spoon.

3. Bake 10 to 12 minutes or until golden brown. Cut into 16 squares. Serve warm or at room temperature. *Makes 16 servings*

SPICY SAUSAGE STUFFED MUSHROOMS

- **24 medium fresh mushrooms, wiped clean**
- **6 ounces sweet Italian sausage, removed from casings (about 2 links)**
- **½ cup chopped green bell pepper**
- **½ cup chopped red onion**
- **¼ cup dry white wine**
- **3 tablespoons FRANK'S® REDHOT® Original Cayenne Pepper Sauce**
- **1 teaspoon Italian seasoning**
- **½ cup (2 ounces) shredded mozzarella cheese**
- **2 tablespoons grated Parmesan cheese**

1. Preheat oven to 400°F. Line baking sheet with foil; grease foil. Remove stems from mushrooms. Chop stems; reserve. Place caps on prepared baking sheet.

2. Heat large nonstick saucepan over medium-high heat. Add sausage; cook and stir 5 minutes or until no longer pink. Drain fat. Add mushroom stems, bell pepper, onion, wine, Frank's RedHot Sauce and Italian seasoning. Bring to a boil. Cook and stir 3 to 5 minutes or until liquid evaporates. Stir in mozzarella cheese.

3. Spoon 1 tablespoon mixture into each mushroom cap, packing slightly. Sprinkle with Parmesan cheese. Bake 10 minutes or until heated through and mushrooms are tender. Serve hot. *Makes 6 servings*

FAST PESTO FOCACCIA

CAPRESE PIZZA

1 loaf (1 pound) frozen pizza or bread dough, thawed
1 container (12 ounces) bruschetta sauce
1 container (8 ounces) pearl-size fresh mozzarella cheese (perlini), drained*

**If pearl-size mozzarella is not available, use one 8-ounce ball of fresh mozzarella and chop into ¼-inch pieces.*

1. Preheat oven to 400°F. Spray jelly-roll pan or baking sheet with nonstick cooking spray.

2. Roll out dough on lightly floured surface into 15×10-inch rectangle. Transfer to prepared pan. Cover loosely with plastic wrap; let rest 10 minutes. Meanwhile, place bruschetta sauce in colander; let drain 10 minutes.

3. Prick surface of dough several times with fork. Bake 10 minutes. Sprinkle with drained bruschetta sauce and top with mozzarella. Bake 10 minutes or until cheese is melted and crust is golden brown. Serve warm.

Makes 6 servings

Tip Bruschetta sauce is a mixture of diced fresh tomatoes, garlic, basil and olive oil. It is typically found in the refrigerated section of the supermarket with other prepared dips such as hummus.

GOAT CHEESE-STUFFED FIGS

7 fresh firm ripe figs
7 slices prosciutto
1 package (4 ounces) goat cheese
Ground black pepper

1. Preheat broiler. Line baking sheet or broiler pan with foil. Cut figs in half vertically. Cut prosciutto slices in half lengthwise to create 14 pieces (about 4 inches long and 1 inch wide).

2. Spread 1 teaspoon goat cheese onto cut side of each fig half. Wrap prosciutto slice around fig and goat cheese. Sprinkle with pepper.

3. Broil about 4 minutes or until cheese softens and figs are heated through.

Makes 14 stuffed figs

PEPPERONI-OREGANO FOCACCIA

1 tablespoon cornmeal
1 package (about 14 ounces) refrigerated pizza dough
½ cup finely chopped pepperoni (about 3 ounces)
1½ teaspoons finely chopped fresh oregano *or* ½ teaspoon dried oregano
2 teaspoons olive oil

1. Preheat oven to 425°F. Spray baking sheet with nonstick cooking spray; sprinkle with cornmeal.

2. Unroll dough on lightly floured surface. Pat dough into 12×9-inch rectangle. Sprinkle half of pepperoni and half of oregano over one side of dough. Fold over dough, making 12×4½-inch rectangle.

3. Roll dough into 12×9-inch rectangle. Place on prepared baking sheet. Prick dough with fork at 2-inch intervals (about 30 times). Brush with oil; sprinkle with remaining pepperoni and oregano.

4. Bake 12 to 15 minutes or until golden brown. (Prick dough several more times if it puffs as it bakes.) Cut into strips.

Makes 12 servings

GOAT CHEESE-STUFFED FIGS

MARGHERITA PANINI BITES

1 loaf (16 ounces) ciabatta or crusty Italian bread, cut into 16 (½-inch) slices
8 teaspoons pesto sauce
16 fresh basil leaves
8 slices mozzarella cheese
24 thin slices plum tomato (about 3 tomatoes)
Olive oil

1. Preheat grill or broiler. Spread one side of 8 bread slices with 1 teaspoon pesto. Top with 2 basil leaves, 1 cheese slice and 3 tomato slices. Top with remaining bread slices.

2. Brush both sides of sandwiches lightly with oil. Grill sandwiches 5 minutes or until lightly browned and cheese is melted, turning once.

3. Cut each sandwich into four pieces. Serve warm. *Makes 32 panini bites*

BELGIOIOSO® FRESH MOZZARELLA CILIEGINE AND GRAPE TOMATO APPETIZER

12 ounces BELGIOIOSO® Fresh Mozzarella Ciliegine
1 pint grape tomatoes
¾ cup Italian vinaigrette
16 small wooden skewers
Freshly ground black pepper and salt

Drain the liquid from the BELGIOIOSO® Fresh Mozzarella Ciliegine, reserving some for storing any leftover cheese. Place the ciliegine in a large bowl. Rinse grape tomatoes well and remove any stems. Drain well and add to bowl with cheese. Add vinaigrette to bowl and toss gently with cheese and tomatoes.

Alternate grape tomatoes and ciliegine on skewers. Sprinkle with black pepper and salt. *Makes 8 servings*

MARGHERITA PANINI BITES

CHICKEN PESTO PIZZA

Cornmeal
1 loaf (16 ounces) frozen bread dough, thawed
1 tablespoon olive oil
8 ounces chicken tenders, cut into ½-inch pieces
½ red onion, thinly sliced
¼ cup pesto sauce
2 large plum tomatoes, seeded and diced
1 cup (4 ounces) shredded pizza cheese blend or mozzarella cheese

1. Preheat oven to 375°F. Sprinkle baking sheet with cornmeal. Roll out dough on lightly floured surface into 14×8-inch rectangle; transfer to prepared baking sheet. Cover loosely with plastic wrap; let rise 20 to 30 minutes in warm place.

2. Heat oil in large skillet over medium heat. Add chicken; cook and stir over 2 minutes. Add onion and pesto; cook and stir 3 to 4 minutes or until chicken is cooked through. Stir in tomatoes. Let cool slightly.

3. Spread chicken mixture evenly over dough to within 1 inch of edges. Sprinkle with cheese.

4. Bake on bottom rack of oven about 20 minutes or until crust is golden brown. Cut into squares.

Makes about 20 appetizer pieces

ITALIAN BREAD WITH TOMATO APPETIZERS

3 medium tomatoes, seeded and finely chopped
2 tablespoons finely chopped red onion
8 tablespoons WISH-BONE® Italian Dressing,* divided
1 tablespoon chopped fresh basil leaves
¼ teaspoon ground black pepper (optional)
1 loaf Italian or French bread (about 18 inches long)

**Also terrific with WISH-BONE® Robusto Italian or Light Italian Dressing.*

1. Combine tomatoes, onion, 2 tablespoons WISH-BONE® Italian Dressing, basil and black pepper in small bowl; set aside.

2. Slice bread diagonally into 18 slices. Brush 1 side of each slice with remaining 6 tablespoons Dressing. Grill or broil bread until golden, turning once. Evenly top grilled slices with tomato mixture.

Makes 18 servings

Tip: The tomato mixture can be prepared ahead.

Prep Time: 15 minutes **Cook Time:** 1 minute

To seed a tomato, cut it in half crosswise. Holding each tomato half over a bowl, cut side down, gently squeeze the tomato to remove the seeds. An alternative method is to remove the seeds with a small spoon.

CARAMELIZED ONION FOCACCIA

2 tablespoons plus 1 teaspoon olive oil, divided
4 onions, cut in half and thinly sliced
½ teaspoon salt
2 tablespoons water
1 tablespoon chopped fresh rosemary
¼ teaspoon black pepper
1 loaf (16 ounces) frozen bread dough, thawed
1 cup (4 ounces) shredded fontina cheese
¼ cup grated Parmesan cheese

1. Heat 2 tablespoons oil in large skillet over medium-high heat. Add onions and salt; cook 10 minutes or until onions begin to brown, stirring occasionally. Stir in water. Reduce heat to medium; partially cover and cook 20 minutes or until onions are deep golden brown, stirring occasionally. Remove from heat; stir in rosemary and pepper. Set aside.

2. Brush 13×9-inch baking pan with remaining 1 teaspoon oil. Roll out dough on lightly floured surface into 13×9-inch rectangle; transfer to prepared pan. Cover; let rise in warm place 30 minutes.

3. Preheat oven to 375°F. Prick dough all over (about 12 times) with fork. Sprinkle fontina over dough; top with caramelized onions. Sprinkle with Parmesan.

4. Bake 18 to 20 minutes or until golden brown. Remove from pan to wire rack. Cut into pieces; serve warm. *Makes 12 servings*

Bruschetta & Crostini

BEANS & SPINACH BRUSCHETTA

1 can (about 15 ounces) Great Northern or cannellini beans, rinsed and drained
4 tablespoons extra virgin olive oil, divided
2 cloves garlic, minced
½ teaspoon salt, divided
½ teaspoon black pepper, divided
6 cups loosely packed spinach, finely chopped
1 tablespoon red wine vinegar
16 slices whole grain baguette

1. Purée beans in food processor. (If necessary add 1 to 2 tablespoons water for a smooth and spreadable texture.) Transfer to medium bowl.

2. Heat 1 tablespoon oil in medium skillet. Add garlic; cook and stir 1 minute. Remove from heat; add ¼ teaspoon salt and ¼ teaspoon pepper. Stir into beans.

3. Heat 1 tablespoon oil in same skillet over medium heat. Add spinach; cook 2 to 3 minutes or until wilted. Stir in vinegar, remaining ¼ teaspoon salt and ¼ teaspoon pepper. Remove from heat.

4. Preheat grill or broiler. Brush baguette slices with remaining 2 tablespoons oil. Grill until bread is golden brown and crisp. Top with bean purée and spinach. Serve immediately.

Makes 16 servings

TWO TOMATO–KALAMATA CROSTINI

8 sun-dried tomatoes (not packed in oil)
1 baguette (4 ounces), cut into 20 (¼-inch-thick) slices
5 ounces grape tomatoes, chopped
12 kalamata olives, pitted and finely chopped
2 teaspoons cider vinegar
1½ teaspoons dried basil
1 teaspoon extra virgin olive oil
⅛ teaspoon salt
1 clove garlic, halved crosswise

1. Preheat oven to 350°F. Place sun-dried tomatoes in medium bowl; cover with boiling water. Let stand 10 minutes. Drain and chop tomatoes.

2. Place bread slices on large baking sheet. Bake 10 minutes or until edges are golden brown. Cool on wire rack.

3. Combine sun-dried tomatoes, grape tomatoes, olives, vinegar, basil, oil and salt in medium bowl; mix well.

4. Rub bread slices with garlic. Top each bread slice with 1 tablespoon tomato mixture.

Makes 20 servings

RED PEPPER ANTIPASTO

1 tablespoon olive oil
3 red bell peppers, cut into 2×¼-inch strips
2 cloves garlic, minced
2 tablespoons red wine vinegar
¼ teaspoon salt
Black pepper
Toasted French bread slices

1. Heat oil in large skillet over medium-high heat. Add bell peppers; cook and stir 8 to 9 minutes or until edges of peppers begin to brown. Reduce heat to medium. Add garlic; cook and stir 1 minute.

2. Add vinegar, salt and black pepper; cook 2 minutes or until all liquid has evaporated. Serve warm or at room temperature with toast.

Makes 6 to 8 servings

RAGÚ® & PESTO BRUSCHETTA

1 loaf French or Italian bread (about 16 inches long), diagonally cut into 1-inch slices
⅓ cup prepared pesto
1 cup RAGÚ® Old World Style® Pasta Sauce, heated
1 cup shredded mozzarella cheese (about 4 ounces)

1. Preheat broiler. On ungreased baking sheet, arrange bread. Broil bread until golden, about 1 minute. Remove from oven.

2. Evenly spread pesto on bread, then evenly top with Pasta Sauce and sprinkle with cheese. Broil until cheese is melted. *Makes 8 servings*

Prep Time: 5 minutes ✦ **Cook Time:** 10 minutes

RED PEPPER ANTIPASTO

ITALIAN SUB CROSTINI

1 loaf (6 inches) French bread, cut into ½-inch slices
Olive oil
1 ball (8 ounces) fresh mozzarella cheese, cut into 12 slices
8 ounces sliced prosciutto
Fresh basil leaves

1. Preheat oven to 400°F. Brush bread slices with oil. Place on ungreased baking sheet. Bake 5 minutes or until crisp.

2. Place one mozzarella slice on each toast; top with one prosciutto slice. Bake 3 minutes or until cheese is melted. Garnish with basil. Serve immediately.

Makes 12 crostini

TUSCAN TUNA CROSTINI

12 thin baguette slices
Olive oil
1 pouch (2.6 ounces) STARKIST® ALBACORE TUNA IN WATER®
2 tablespoons light mayonnaise
2 teaspoons fresh lemon juice
1 small clove garlic, minced
1½ tablespoons sun-dried tomato spread

1. Preheat oven to 425°F.

2. Brush bread slices lightly with olive oil. Place on baking sheet. Bake at 425°F for 10 minutes or until lightly toasted.

3. Combine tuna, mayonnaise, lemon juice and garlic.

4. Spread sun-dried tomato spread over crostini.

5. Top with tuna mixture and garnish with fresh basil and red and yellow pepper strips, if desired.

Makes 12 crostini

Tip: If you cannot find prepared sun-dried tomato spread, make your own! Place 3 to 4 sun-dried tomatoes in boiling water and let soak until softened. Take them out of the water and mash with a fork or purée them in a mini food chopper.

BRUSCHETTA

3 teaspoons olive oil, divided
½ cup thinly sliced onion
1 cup chopped seeded tomato
2 tablespoons capers, drained
½ teaspoon salt
¼ teaspoon black pepper
3 cloves garlic, minced
4 slices French bread
½ cup (2 ounces) shredded Monterey Jack cheese

1. Heat 2 teaspoons oil in large nonstick skillet over medium heat. Add onion; cook and stir 5 minutes. Stir in tomato, capers, salt and pepper; cook 3 minutes.

2. Preheat broiler. Combine garlic and remaining 1 teaspoon oil in small bowl; brush over bread slices. Top with onion mixture; sprinkle with Monterey Jack. Place on baking sheet. Broil 3 minutes or until cheese melts.

Makes 4 servings

ARTICHOKE CROSTINI

1 jar (about 6 ounces) marinated artichoke hearts, drained and chopped
3 green onions, chopped
5 tablespoons grated Parmesan cheese, divided
2 tablespoons mayonnaise
12 slices French bread (½ inch thick)

1. Preheat broiler. Combine artichokes, green onions, 3 tablespoons Parmesan and mayonnaise in small bowl; mix well.

2. Arrange bread slices on baking sheet. Broil 4 to 5 inches from heat 2 to 3 minutes per side or until lightly browned.

3. Spread about 1 tablespoon artichoke mixture on each bread slice; sprinkle with remaining 2 tablespoons Parmesan. Broil 1 to 2 minutes or until cheese is melted and lightly browned.

Makes 12 crostini

TUSCAN WHITE BEAN CROSTINI

2 cans (about 15 ounces each) cannellini or Great Northern beans, rinsed and drained
½ large red bell pepper, finely chopped *or* ⅓ cup finely chopped roasted red bell pepper
⅓ cup finely chopped onion
⅓ cup red wine vinegar
3 tablespoons chopped fresh parsley
1 tablespoon olive oil
2 cloves garlic, minced
½ teaspoon salt
½ teaspoon dried oregano
¼ teaspoon black pepper
18 slices French bread, about ¼ inch thick

1. Combine beans, bell pepper and onion in large bowl.

2. Whisk vinegar, parsley, oil, garlic, salt, oregano and black pepper in small bowl until well blended. Pour over bean mixture; toss to coat. Cover and refrigerate 2 hours or overnight.

3. Preheat broiler. Arrange bread slices in single layer on large ungreased baking sheet or broiler pan. Broil 6 to 8 inches from heat 30 to 45 seconds or until bread slices are lightly toasted. Cool completely.

4. Top each bread slice with bean mixture. *Makes 18 crostini*

CROSTINI WITH LEMONY PESTO

1 baguette (4 ounces)
3 tablespoons pesto sauce
1 teaspoon lemon juice
½ cup chopped plum tomato

1. Preheat oven to 350°F.

2. Cut baguette crosswise into 16 slices; arrange on baking sheet. Bake 11 to 12 minutes or until bread begins to brown. Cool completely.

3. Combine pesto and lemon juice in small bowl; stir until well blended. Spread ½ teaspoon pesto mixture on each bread slice. Top with tomato. Serve immediately. *Makes 16 crostini*

MUSHROOM PARMESAN CROSTINI

1 tablespoon olive oil
1 clove garlic, finely chopped
1 cup chopped mushrooms
1 loaf Italian or French bread (about 12 inches long), cut into 12 slices and toasted
¾ cup RAGÚ® Pizza Quick® Snack Sauce
¼ cup grated Parmesan cheese
1 tablespoon finely chopped fresh basil leaves *or* 1 teaspoon dried basil leaves

1. Preheat oven to 375°F. In 8-inch nonstick skillet, heat olive oil over medium heat and cook garlic 30 seconds. Add mushrooms and cook, stirring occasionally, 2 minutes or until liquid evaporates.

2. On baking sheet, arrange bread slices. Evenly spread Snack Sauce on bread slices, then top with mushroom mixture, cheese and basil. Bake 15 minutes or until heated through. *Makes 12 crostini*

Recipe Tip: Many varieties of mushrooms are available in supermarkets and specialty grocery stores. Shiitake, portobello and cremini mushrooms all have excellent flavor.

TOMATO & CAPER CROSTINI

1 French roll, cut into 8 slices
2 plum tomatoes, finely chopped
1½ tablespoons capers, drained
1½ teaspoons dried basil
1 teaspoon extra virgin olive oil
¼ cup (1 ounce) crumbled feta cheese with sun-dried tomatoes and basil (or any variety)

1. Preheat oven to 350°F.

2. Place bread slices in single layer on ungreased baking sheet. Bake 15 minutes or until golden brown. Cool completely.

3. Meanwhile, combine tomatoes, capers, basil and oil in small bowl; mix well. Just before serving, spoon about 1 tablespoon tomato mixture on each bread slice; sprinkle with feta. *Makes 4 servings*

WARM TOMATO & OLIVE BRUSCHETTA

12 slices (½ inch thick) whole wheat French baguette
36 sprays I CAN'T BELIEVE IT'S NOT BUTTER!® Spray Original
½ teaspoon LAWRY'S® Garlic Powder With Parsley
2 small plum tomatoes, finely chopped (about ⅔ cup)
2 tablespoons finely chopped kalamata olives
1 tablespoon grated Parmesan cheese

Preheat oven to 400°F.

Spray each bread slice 2 times with I CAN'T BELIEVE IT'S NOT BUTTER!® Spray Original, then evenly sprinkle with Garlic Powder. Bake 4 minutes or until slightly toasted.

In small bowl, combine tomatoes with olives. Top each bread slice with tomato mixture, then spray once with Spray. Bake 4 minutes or until warm. Evenly sprinkle with cheese and, if desired, ground black pepper. Serve warm. *Makes 4 servings*

Prep Time: 10 minutes ✣ **Cook Time:** 8 minutes

BEANS & GREENS CROSTINI

4 tablespoons olive oil, divided
1 small onion, thinly sliced
4 cups thinly sliced Italian black kale or other dinosaur kale variety
2 tablespoons minced garlic, divided
1 tablespoon balsamic vinegar
2 teaspoons salt, divided
¼ teaspoon red pepper flakes
1 can (about 15 ounces) cannellini beans, rinsed and drained
1 tablespoon chopped fresh rosemary
Toasted baguette slices

1. Heat 1 tablespoon oil in large nonstick skillet over medium heat. Add onion; cook and stir 5 minutes or until softened. Add kale and 1 tablespoon garlic; cook and stir 15 minutes or until kale is softened and most of liquid has evaporated. Stir in vinegar, 1 teaspoon salt and red pepper flakes.

2. Meanwhile, combine beans, remaining 3 tablespoons olive oil, 1 tablespoon garlic, rosemary and remaining 1 teaspoon salt in food processor; process until smooth.

3. Spread baguette slices with bean mixture; top with kale.

Makes about 24 crostini

Tip: Store kale in a plastic bag in the refrigerator. Use it within two or three days; its flavor becomes stronger if stored longer.

Small Plates

CAPRESE–STYLE TARTLETS

3 tomatoes, cut into 4 slices each
3 tablespoons pesto sauce
1 sheet frozen puff pastry, thawed
6 ounces fresh mozzarella cheese
2 tablespoons chopped kalamata olives

1. Place in tomatoes in resealable food storage bag. Add pesto; toss to coat. Marinate at room temperature 30 minutes.

2. Preheat oven to 425°F. Line baking sheet with parchment paper. Cut out six 4-inch rounds from pastry; place on prepared baking sheet. Top each round with two tomato slices. Bake 12 minutes or until pastry is light golden and puffed.

3. Preheat broiler. Cut mozzarella into six ¼-inch-thick slices. Top each tart with one mozzarella slice. Broil 1 minute or until cheese is melted. Top tarts evenly with olives. Serve warm. *Makes 6 tartlets*

TOMATO & CHEESE FOCACCIA

1 package (¼ ounce) active dry yeast
¾ cup warm water (105° to 115°F)
2 cups all-purpose flour
½ teaspoon salt
4 tablespoons olive oil, divided
1 teaspoon Italian seasoning
8 oil-packed sun-dried tomatoes, well drained
½ cup (2 ounces) shredded provolone cheese
¼ cup grated Parmesan cheese

1. Dissolve yeast in warm water in small bowl; let stand 5 minutes. Combine flour and salt in food processor. Add yeast mixture and 3 tablespoons oil; process until ingredients form a ball. Process 1 minute.

2. Turn dough out onto lightly floured surface. Knead about 2 minutes or until smooth and elastic. Place dough in oiled bowl; turn dough over to grease top. Cover; let rise in warm place about 30 minutes or until doubled.

3. Punch down dough. Let rest 5 minutes. Press dough into oiled 10-inch round baking pan, deep-dish pizza pan or springform pan. Brush with remaining 1 tablespoon oil; sprinkle with Italian seasoning. Press sun-dried tomatoes into top of dough; sprinkle with provolone and Parmesan. Cover; let rise in warm place 15 minutes.

4. Preheat oven to 425°F. Bake 20 to 25 minutes or until golden brown. Cut into wedges to serve.

Makes 1 loaf (6 to 8 servings)

Note: If mixing dough by hand, combine flour and salt in large bowl. Stir in yeast mixture and 3 tablespoons oil until a ball forms. Turn out onto lightly floured surface and knead about 10 minutes or until smooth and elastic. Proceed as directed.

Serving Suggestion: Serve with rosemary-infused olive oil for dipping.

CLAMS DIABLO

2 tablespoons olive or vegetable oil
½ cup chopped onion
1 clove garlic, minced
1 can (14.5 ounces) CONTADINA® Diced Tomatoes, undrained
¼ cup dry red wine or chicken broth
½ teaspoon dried thyme leaves, crushed
¼ teaspoon salt
¼ teaspoon crushed red pepper flakes
1½ pounds scrubbed fresh clams
2 tablespoons chopped fresh parsley *or* 2 teaspoons dried parsley flakes

1. Heat oil in medium skillet. Add onion and garlic; sauté for 1 minute.

2. Stir in undrained tomatoes, wine, thyme, salt and red pepper flakes. Bring to a boil.

3. Reduce heat to low; simmer, uncovered, for 10 minutes, stirring occasionally.

4. Add clams; cover. Simmer for 5 minutes or just until clams open. Sprinkle with parsley just before serving.

Makes about 4 to 6 servings

Prep Time: 8 minutes **Cook Time:** 17 minutes

POLENTA APPETIZERS

1 package (16 ounces) prepared basil and garlic flavored polenta
½ cup pasta sauce
¼ to ⅓ cup garlic and herb spreadable cheese

1. Cut polenta into ¼-inch-thick slices.

2. Spray large skillet with nonstick cooking spray; heat over medium heat. Cook polenta slices 3 minutes per side or until lightly browned. Remove to serving plate; cool slightly.

3. Meanwhile, place pasta sauce in small microwavable bowl. Cover with vented plastic wrap. Microwave on HIGH about 1 minute or until heated through. Top polenta rounds with 1 teaspoon pasta sauce and ½ teaspoon cheese.

Makes about 16 appetizers (4 to 6 servings)

Tip

If flavored polenta is not available, you can substitute plain polenta. For additional flavor, add 1 small clove garlic, minced, and 1 tablespoon chopped fresh basil to the pasta sauce before heating it.

ROASTED EGGPLANT SPREAD WITH FOCACCIA

1 eggplant (1 pound)
1 medium tomato
1 tablespoon fresh lemon juice
1 tablespoon chopped fresh basil *or* 1 teaspoon dried basil
2 teaspoons chopped fresh thyme *or* ¾ teaspoon dried thyme
1 clove garlic, minced
¼ teaspoon salt
1 tablespoon extra virgin olive oil
Focaccia (recipe follows)

1. Preheat oven to 400°F. Poke holes in several places in eggplant with fork. Place eggplant on oven rack; bake 10 minutes. Cut stem end from tomato; place in small baking pan. Place tomato in oven with eggplant. Bake vegetables 40 minutes.

2. Cool vegetables slightly; peel. Coarsely chop eggplant. Place tomato, eggplant, lemon juice, basil, thyme, garlic and salt in food processor; process until well blended. With motor running, slowly drizzle oil through feed tube and process until well blended. Refrigerate 3 hours or overnight.

3. Prepare Focaccia; serve with eggplant spread. *Makes 10 servings*

FOCACCIA

1½ teaspoons sugar
1 teaspoon active dry yeast
¾ cup warm water (110° to 115°F)
1 tablespoon plus 1 teaspoon extra virgin olive oil, divided
1 teaspoon salt
1 teaspoon dried rosemary
1 cup all-purpose flour
1 cup whole wheat flour

continued on page 62

Focaccia, continued

1. Stir sugar and yeast into water in large bowl until dissolved. Let stand 10 minutes or until bubbly. Stir in 1 tablespoon oil, salt and rosemary. Add flours, ½ cup at a time, stirring until dough begins to pull away from side of bowl and forms a ball.

2. Turn dough out onto lightly floured surface; knead 5 minutes or until smooth and elastic, adding more flour if necessary. Place dough in oiled bowl; turn dough over to grease top. Cover; let rise in warm place 1 hour or until doubled.

3. Turn dough onto lightly floured surface; knead 1 minute. Divide dough into 3 balls; roll each into 6-inch circle. Make indentations in dough with fingertips. Place on greased baking sheet. Cover; let rise 30 minutes.

4. Preheat oven to 400°F. Brush tops of dough circles with remaining 1 teaspoon oil. Bake about 13 minutes or until golden brown. Cut each loaf into 10 wedges. *Makes 10 servings (30 wedges)*

ASPARAGUS & PROSCIUTTO ANTIPASTO

12 asparagus spears (about 8 ounces)
2 ounces cream cheese, softened
¼ cup (1 ounce) crumbled blue cheese or goat cheese
¼ teaspoon black pepper
1 package (3 to 4 ounces) thinly sliced prosciutto

1. Trim and discard tough ends of asparagus. Simmer asparagus in salted water in large skillet 4 to 5 minutes or until crisp-tender. Drain and rinse with cold water until cool. Drain and pat dry with paper towels.

2. Combine cream cheese, blue cheese and pepper in small bowl; mix well. Cut prosciutto slices in half crosswise to make 12 pieces. Spread cream cheese mixture evenly over one side of each prosciutto slice.

3. Wrap each asparagus spear with prosciutto slice. Serve at room temperature or slightly chilled. *Makes 12 appetizers*

BALSAMIC ONION & PROSCIUTTO PIZZETTES

- **1 package (16 ounces) refrigerated pizza dough***
- **2 tablespoons extra virgin olive oil, divided**
- **1 large or 2 small red onions, cut in half and thinly sliced**
- **¼ teaspoon salt**
- **1½ tablespoons balsamic vinegar**
- **⅛ teaspoon black pepper**
- **⅔ cup grated Parmesan cheese**
- **4 ounces fresh mozzarella, cut into small pieces**
- **1 package (about 3 ounces) thinly sliced prosciutto, cut or torn into small pieces**

**Frozen pizza dough can also be used. Thaw according to package directions.*

1. Remove dough from refrigerator; let rest at room temperature while preparing onions. Heat 1 tablespoon oil in medium skillet over medium-high heat. Add onion and salt; cook about 20 minutes or until tender and golden brown, stirring occasionally. Stir in vinegar and pepper; cook and stir 2 minutes. Set aside to cool.

2. Preheat oven to 450°F. Line two baking sheets with parchment paper.

3. Divide dough into 16 balls; press each into 3-inch round (about ⅜-inch thick) on prepared baking sheets. Brush dough with remaining 1 tablespoon oil; sprinkle each piece with about 1 teaspoon Parmesan. Top with cooked onion, mozzarella, prosciutto and remaining Parmesan.

4. Bake about 13 minutes or until crusts are golden brown.

Makes 16 pizzettes

EGGPLANT PARMESAN ANTIPASTI

3 tablespoons extra virgin olive oil, divided
1 clove garlic, minced
¼ teaspoon dried oregano
1 can (about 15 ounces) crushed tomatoes
¾ teaspoon salt, divided
6 fresh basil leaves, torn into small pieces
1 medium or 2 small eggplants* (about 1 pound)
½ teaspoon black pepper, divided
½ cup grated Parmesan cheese
4 to 6 ounces fresh mozzarella, cut into thin (⅛-inch) slices
Additional fresh basil leaves, chopped (optional)

**Choose eggplant about 2½ to 3 inches in diameter to create smaller slices; avoid very large or bulbous eggplants.*

1. Preheat broiler. Line large rimmed baking sheet with foil. Brush foil with 2 teaspoons oil.

2. Heat 1 tablespoon oil in medium saucepan. Add garlic and oregano; cook and stir over medium heat about 1 minute or just until garlic becomes fragrant. Add tomatoes and ¼ teaspoon salt; bring to a simmer. Simmer about 15 minutes; stir in basil.

3. Meanwhile, cut eggplant crosswise into ½-inch slices. Arrange eggplant on prepared baking sheet; brush with 2 teaspoons oil. Sprinkle with remaining ½ teaspoon salt and ¼ teaspoon pepper.

4. Broil 4 to 6 inches from heat source about 7 minutes or until well browned. Turn eggplant; brush with remaining 2 teaspoons oil and sprinkle with remaining ¼ teaspoon pepper. Broil about 6 minutes or until well browned.

5. Sprinkle each eggplant slice with 1 teaspoon Parmesan. Top with 1 tablespoon sauce, 1 mozzarella slice and 1 teaspoon Parmesan. Broil about 3 minutes or until cheese is bubbly and just beginning to brown. Sprinkle with chopped basil, if desired. Serve immediately. *Makes 4 to 6 servings*

Note: Refrigerate or freeze leftover tomato sauce for another use, such as pizza or pasta.

ANTIPASTI FOCACCIA SALAD

Dressing

- **½ cup extra virgin olive oil**
- **3 tablespoons red wine vinegar**
- **2 teaspoons dried basil**
- **1½ teaspoons dried oregano**
- **1 medium clove garlic, minced**
- **½ teaspoon salt**
- **⅛ teaspoon red pepper flakes**

Salad

- **½ round loaf focaccia, cut into 4 wedges**
- **2 medium tomatoes, cut into 4 slices each**
- **1 can (7 ounces) hearts of palm, drained and sliced**
- **5 ounces romaine lettuce**
- **8 slices hard salami, cut into thin strips**
- **2 ounces fresh mozzarella, cut into ½-inch cubes**
- **8 jumbo stuffed green olives**

1. Combine dressing ingredients in jar with tight-fitting lid; cover and shake until well blended.

2. Spoon 1 tablespoon dressing evenly over each focaccia wedge; let soak into bread. Top each wedge with two tomato slices.

3. Combine hearts of palm, romaine, salami, mozzarella and olives in large bowl. Add remaining dressing; toss to coat. Serve over focaccia wedges.

Makes 4 servings

Variation: Add 1 can (about 15 ounces) chickpeas, rinsed and drained, to the salad.

OYSTERS ROMANO

12 oysters, shucked and on the half shell
2 slices bacon, cut into 6 pieces each
½ cup Italian seasoned dry bread crumbs
2 tablespoons butter, melted
½ teaspoon garlic salt
6 tablespoons grated Romano or Parmesan cheese
Fresh chives (optional)

1. Preheat oven to 375°F. Place shells with oysters on baking sheet. Top each oyster with one bacon piece. Bake 10 minutes or until bacon is crisp.

2. Combine bread crumbs, butter and garlic salt in small bowl. Spoon mixture over oysters; sprinkle with Romano. Bake 5 minutes or until cheese is melted. Garnish with chives.

Makes 12 oysters

SKEWERED ANTIPASTO

1 jar (8 ounces) SONOMA® Marinated Dried Tomatoes
1 pound (3 medium) new potatoes, cooked until tender
2 cups bite-sized vegetable pieces (such as celery, bell peppers, radishes, carrots, cucumber and green onions)
1 cup drained cooked egg tortellini and/or spinach tortellini
1 tablespoon chopped fresh chives *or* 1 teaspoon dried chives
1 tablespoon chopped fresh rosemary leaves *or* 1 teaspoon dried rosemary

Drain oil from tomatoes into medium bowl. Place tomatoes in small bowl; set aside. Cut potatoes into 1-inch cubes. Add potatoes, vegetables, tortellini, chives and rosemary to oil in medium bowl. Stir to coat with oil; cover and marinate 1 hour at room temperature. To assemble, alternately thread tomatoes, potatoes, vegetables and tortellini onto 6-inch skewers.

Makes 12 to 14 skewers

OYSTERS ROMANO

QUICK & EASY RAVIOLI SOUP

½ pound mild Italian sausage, casings removed
½ cup chopped onion
1 clove garlic, crushed
2 cans (about 14 ounces each) chicken broth
2 cups water
1 package (9 ounces) frozen mini cheese-filled ravioli
1 can (about 15 ounces) chickpeas, rinsed and drained
1 can (about 14 ounces) diced tomatoes
¾ teaspoon dried oregano
½ teaspoon black pepper
1 cup fresh baby spinach
Grated Parmesan cheese

1. Cook sausage, onion and garlic in large saucepan or Dutch oven over medium heat 5 minutes, stirring to break up meat. Drain fat. Remove sausage mixture to bowl.

2. Add broth and water to saucepan; bring to a boil over medium-high heat. Add ravioli; cook 4 to 5 minutes or until tender.

3. Stir in sausage mixture, chickpeas, tomatoes, oregano and pepper; heat through. Stir in spinach; cook 1 minute or until wilted. Sprinkle with Parmesan just before serving.
Makes 8 servings

TOMATO–FRESH MOZZARELLA SALAD

Vinaigrette Dressing (recipe follows)
1 pound fresh mozzarella cheese
1 pound ripe tomatoes
Fresh basil leaves
Salt and black pepper

Prepare Vinaigrette Dressing. Cut mozzarella into ¼-inch slices. Cut tomatoes into ¼-inch slices. Arrange mozzarella slices, tomato slices and basil leaves overlapping on plate. Drizzle with dressing. Sprinkle with salt and pepper.

Makes 4 servings

VINAIGRETTE DRESSING

1 tablespoon balsamic vinegar or red wine vinegar
¼ teaspoon Dijon mustard
Pinch *each* sugar, salt and pepper
¼ cup extra virgin olive oil

Combine vinegar, mustard, sugar, salt and pepper in small bowl; whisk until smooth. Add oil in thin stream, whisking until smooth. Refrigerate until ready to use. Whisk again before serving.

Makes about ¼ cup dressing

GREEN BEAN SALAD

1 pound fresh green beans, trimmed
3 tablespoons lemon juice
1 tablespoon FILIPPO BERIO® Extra Virgin Olive Oil
½ teaspoon dried oregano leaves
Salt

In medium saucepan, cook beans in boiling salted water 10 to 15 minutes or until tender. Drain well; cool slightly. In small bowl, whisk together lemon juice, olive oil and oregano. Pour over green beans; toss until lightly coated. Cover; refrigerate several hours or overnight before serving. Season to taste with salt.

Makes 6 servings

ITALIAN MUSHROOM SOUP

½ cup dried porcini mushrooms (about ½ ounce)
1 tablespoon olive oil
2 cups chopped onions
8 ounces sliced cremini or button mushrooms
2 cloves garlic, minced
¼ teaspoon dried thyme
¼ cup all-purpose flour
4 cups vegetable broth
½ cup whipping cream
⅓ cup Marsala wine (optional)
Salt and black pepper

1. Place dried mushrooms in small bowl; cover with boiling water. Let stand 15 minutes or until tender.

2. Meanwhile, heat oil in large saucepan over medium heat. Add onions; cook 5 minutes or until translucent, stirring occasionally. Add cremini mushrooms, garlic and thyme; cook 8 minutes, stirring occasionally. Add flour; cook and stir 1 minute. Stir in broth.

3. Drain porcini mushrooms, reserving liquid. Chop mushrooms; add to saucepan with reserved liquid. Bring to a boil. Reduce heat to medium-low; simmer 10 minutes.

4. Stir in cream and Marsala, if desired. Season with salt and pepper. Simmer 5 minutes or until heated through. Serve immediately.

Makes 6 to 8 servings

WHITE BEAN & ORZO SALAD

¾ cup uncooked orzo pasta (6 ounces)
1 can (about 15 ounces) navy beans, rinsed and drained
1 cup packed spinach leaves, coarsely chopped
½ cup chopped roasted red peppers
3 tablespoons capers, drained and rinsed
3 tablespoons chopped fresh basil
3 tablespoons Italian dressing
¼ cup crumbled feta cheese

1. Cook pasta according to package directions.

2. Combine beans, spinach, roasted peppers, capers, basil and dressing in large bowl.

3. Drain pasta; add to bean mixture. Add feta and toss gently.

Makes 6 servings

SICILIAN-STYLE PASTA SALAD

1 pound dry rotini pasta
2 cans (14.5 ounces each) CONTADINA® Diced Tomatoes with Italian Herbs, undrained
1 cup sliced yellow bell pepper
1 cup sliced zucchini
8 ounces cooked bay shrimp
1 can (2¼ ounces) sliced pitted ripe olives, drained
2 tablespoons balsamic vinegar

1. Cook pasta according to package directions; drain.

2. Combine pasta, undrained tomatoes, bell pepper, zucchini, shrimp, olives and vinegar in large bowl; toss well.

3. Cover. Chill before serving.

Makes 10 servings

WHITE BEAN & ORZO SALAD ▶

ITALIAN SKILLET ROASTED VEGETABLE SOUP

2 tablespoons olive oil, divided
1 medium red, yellow or orange bell pepper, chopped
1 clove garlic, minced
2 cups water
1 can (about 14 ounces) diced tomatoes
1 medium zucchini, thinly sliced lengthwise
⅛ teaspoon red pepper flakes
1 can (about 15 ounces) navy beans, rinsed and drained
3 to 4 tablespoons chopped fresh basil
1 tablespoon balsamic vinegar
¾ teaspoon salt

1. Heat 1 tablespoon oil in deep skillet over medium-high heat. Add bell pepper; cook and stir 4 minutes or until edges are browned. Add garlic; cook and stir 15 seconds.

2. Add water, tomatoes, zucchini and red pepper flakes; bring to a boil over high heat. Reduce heat to medium-low; cover and simmer 20 minutes.

3. Add beans, basil, remaining 1 tablespoon oil, vinegar and salt; simmer about 2 minutes. Remove from heat; let stand, covered, 10 minutes before serving.

Makes 4 to 6 servings

FENNEL, OLIVE & RADICCHIO SALAD

½ cup Italian- or Greek-style black olives, divided
¼ cup extra virgin olive oil
1 tablespoon lemon juice
1 flat anchovy fillet *or* ½ teaspoon anchovy paste
¼ teaspoon salt
Dash black pepper
Pinch sugar
1 bulb fennel
1 head radicchio*
Fennel tops (optional)

**Radicchio, a tart red chicory, is available in large supermarkets and specialty food shops. If it is not available, substitute 2 heads of Belgian endive. Although it does not provide the dramatic red color, it will provide a similar texture, and its slightly bitter flavor will go well with the robust dressing and the sweet anise flavor of the fennel.*

1. For dressing, cut 3 olives in half; remove and discard pits. Place pitted olives, oil, lemon juice and anchovy in food processor or blender; process 5 seconds. Add salt, pepper and sugar; process about 5 seconds or until olives are finely chopped. Set aside.

2. Cut off and discard fennel stalks, reserving green leafy tops for garnish. Cut off and discard root end of bulb and any discolored parts of bulb. Cut fennel bulb lengthwise into 8 wedges; separate each wedge into segments.

3. Separate radicchio leaves; rinse thoroughly. Drain well.

4. Arrange radicchio leaves, fennel and remaining olives on serving plate. Spoon dressing over salad; garnish with fennel leaves. Serve immediately.

Makes 4 servings

TUSCAN WHITE BEAN SOUP

10 cups chicken broth
1 package (16 ounces) dried Great Northern beans, rinsed and sorted
1 can (about 14 ounces) diced tomatoes
1 large onion, chopped
3 carrots, chopped
6 ounces bacon, crisp-cooked and diced
4 cloves garlic, minced
1 fresh rosemary sprig *or* 1 teaspoon dried rosemary
1 teaspoon black pepper

Slow Cooker Directions

1. Combine broth, beans, tomatoes, onion, carrots, bacon, garlic, rosemary and pepper in 5-quart slow cooker.

2. Cover; cook on LOW 8 hours. Remove and discard rosemary before serving.

Makes 8 to 10 servings

Serving Suggestion: Place slices of toasted Italian bread in bottom of individual soup bowls. Drizzle with olive oil. Ladle soup over bread.

SIMPLE MEATBALL SOUP

1 package (15 to 18 ounces) frozen Italian sausage meatballs without sauce
2 cans (about 14 ounces each) Italian-style stewed tomatoes
2 cans (about 14 ounces each) beef broth
1 can (about 14 ounces) mixed vegetables
½ cup uncooked rotini pasta or small macaroni
½ teaspoon dried oregano

1. Thaw meatballs in microwave according to package directions.

2. Place remaining ingredients in large saucepan. Add meatballs; bring to a boil. Reduce heat to medium-low; cover and simmer 15 minutes or until pasta is tender.

Makes 4 to 6 servings

GRILLED TRI–COLORED PEPPER SALAD

- **1 *each* large red, yellow and green bell pepper, cut into halves or quarters**
- **⅓ cup extra virgin olive oil**
- **3 tablespoons balsamic vinegar**
- **2 cloves garlic, minced**
- **¼ teaspoon salt**
- **¼ teaspoon black pepper**
- **⅓ cup crumbled goat cheese (about 1½ ounces)**
- **¼ cup thinly sliced fresh basil leaves**

1. Prepare grill for direct cooking over high heat.

2. Place bell peppers, skin side down, on grid. Grill, covered, 10 to 12 minutes or until skin is charred. Transfer to paper bag. Close bag; let stand 10 to 15 minutes. Remove and discard skin.

3. Place bell peppers in shallow serving dish. Combine oil, vinegar, garlic, salt and black pepper in small bowl; whisk until well blended. Pour over bell peppers. Let stand 30 minutes at room temperature. (Or cover and refrigerate up to 24 hours. Bring bell peppers to room temperature before serving.)

4. Sprinkle with goat cheese and basil just before serving.

Makes 4 to 6 servings

Peppers should be firm and feel heavy for their size with bright shiny skins and hard green stems. Avoid peppers that have wrinkles, soft spots or bruises. Store unwashed sweet peppers in the refrigerator. Green peppers begin to lose their crispness after three to four days, and red peppers are even more perishable.

ITALIAN WEDDING SOUP

1 tablespoon olive oil
1 pound bulk Italian sausage*
½ cup chopped onion
½ cup chopped carrots
1 teaspoon Italian seasoning
7½ cups chicken broth
3 cups packed coarsely chopped kale
1 cup uncooked ditalini or other small shaped pasta
Grated Parmesan cheese (optional)

**If bulk sausage is not available, use sausage links and remove the casings.*

1. Heat oil in large saucepan over medium-high heat. Add sausage, onion, carrots and Italian seasoning; cook and stir about 4 minutes or until sausage is cooked through. Drain fat.

2. Stir in broth and kale; bring to a boil over high heat. Stir in pasta. Reduce heat to medium-low; simmer, partially covered, about 9 minutes or until pasta is tender. Sprinkle with Parmesan. *Makes 6 servings*

MINESTRONE SALAD

1 can (about 15 ounces) chickpeas, rinsed and drained
1 large tomato, chopped
2 stalks celery, chopped
1 cup cooked macaroni
¼ cup grated Parmesan cheese
2 tablespoons Italian dressing
Salt and black pepper

Combine chickpeas, tomato, celery, macaroni, Parmesan and dressing in large bowl; mix well. Season with salt and pepper. *Makes 4 servings*

FRESH TOMATO PASTA SOUP

1 tablespoon olive oil
½ cup chopped onion
1 clove garlic, minced
3 pounds fresh tomatoes (about 9 medium), coarsely chopped
3 cups vegetable or chicken broth
1 tablespoon minced fresh basil
1 tablespoon minced fresh marjoram
1 tablespoon minced fresh oregano
1 teaspoon whole fennel seeds
½ teaspoon black pepper
¾ cup uncooked rosamarina, orzo or other small pasta
½ cup (2 ounces) shredded mozzarella cheese

1. Heat oil in large saucepan over medium heat. Add onion and garlic; cook and stir until onion is tender.

2. Add tomatoes, broth, basil, marjoram, oregano, fennel seeds and pepper; bring to a boil. Reduce heat to low; cover and simmer 25 minutes. Remove from heat; cool slightly.

3. Purée soup in batches in food processor or blender Return to saucepan; bring to a boil.

4. Add pasta; cook 7 to 9 minutes or until tender. Sprinkle with mozzarella.

Makes 8 servings

SWEET ITALIAN MARINATED VEGETABLE SALAD

- ½ (14-ounce) can quartered artichoke hearts, drained
- 5 ounces grape or cherry tomatoes, halved
- ½ cup chopped green bell pepper
- ¼ cup finely chopped red onion
- 2 ounces mozzarella cheese, cut into ¼-inch cubes
- 2 tablespoons white wine vinegar
- 1 tablespoon chopped fresh oregano *or* 1 teaspoon dried oregano
- 2 teaspoons sugar
- ⅛ teaspoon salt
- ⅛ teaspoon red pepper flakes

Combine all ingredients in medium bowl; toss to coat. Serve immediately or refrigerate 1 hour to allow flavors to blend. *Makes 4 servings*

PANZANELLA (ITALIAN BREAD SALAD)

- 4 ounces day-old French bread, cubed*
- 4 plum tomatoes, chopped
- 3 tablespoons extra virgin olive oil
- 2 tablespoons red wine vinegar
- 1 clove garlic, minced
- ½ teaspoon salt
- ¼ cup chopped fresh basil

**You can substitute day-old whole wheat bread, sourdough bread or pita bread for the French bread. Cube it or tear it into small pieces.*

1. Combine bread cubes and tomatoes in serving bowl.

2. Whisk oil, vinegar, garlic and salt in small bowl; stir in basil. Pour over bread mixture; toss to coat. *Makes 6 servings*

PASTA E FAGIOLI

2 tablespoons olive oil
1 cup chopped onion
3 cloves garlic, minced
2 cans (about 14 ounces each) Italian-style stewed tomatoes, undrained
3 cups vegetable or chicken broth
1 can (about 15 ounces) cannellini beans or Great Northern beans, undrained
¼ cup chopped fresh Italian parsley
1 teaspoon dried basil
¼ teaspoon black pepper
4 ounces uncooked small shell pasta

1. Heat oil in large saucepan or Dutch oven over medium heat. Add onion and garlic; cook and stir 5 minutes or until onion is tender.

2. Add tomatoes, broth, beans with liquid, parsley, basil and pepper; bring to a boil over high heat, stirring occasionally. Reduce heat to low; cover and simmer 10 minutes.

3. Add pasta; cover and simmer 10 minutes or just until pasta is tender. Serve immediately.

Makes 8 servings

MIXED SPRING VEGETABLE SALAD

8 ounces fresh green beans, trimmed and cut into thirds
1 medium zucchini (about ½ pound), sliced
1 large tomato *or* 3 plum tomatoes, sliced
3 tablespoons FILIPPO BERIO® Extra Virgin Olive Oil
3 tablespoons lemon juice
Salt and freshly ground black pepper

Cook or steam green beans and zucchini separately until tender-crisp. Cover; refrigerate until chilled. Stir in tomato. Just before serving, drizzle olive oil and lemon juice over vegetables. Season to taste with salt and pepper.

Makes 6 servings

PASTA & RISOTTO

Table of Contents

Classic Pasta

CLASSIC FETTUCCINE ALFREDO

12 ounces uncooked fettuccine
⅔ cup whipping cream
6 tablespoons unsalted butter
½ teaspoon salt
Generous dash white pepper
Generous dash ground nutmeg
1 cup grated Parmesan cheese
2 tablespoons chopped fresh Italian parsley

1. Cook pasta according to package directions; drain and keep warm in saucepan.

2. Heat cream and butter in large heavy skillet over medium-low heat until butter melts and mixture bubbles, stirring frequently. Cook and stir 2 minutes. Stir in salt, pepper and nutmeg. Remove from heat; gradually stir in Parmesan until well blended and smooth. Return to low heat, if necessary; do not let sauce bubble or cheese will become lumpy and tough.

3. Pour sauce over pasta. Cook and stir over low heat 2 to 3 minutes or until sauce is thickened and pasta is evenly coated. Sprinkle with parsley. Serve immediately. *Makes 4 servings*

QUICK PASTA PUTTANESCA

16 ounces uncooked spaghetti or linguine
3 tablespoons plus 1 teaspoon olive oil, divided
¼ to 1 teaspoon red pepper flakes*
1 tablespoon dried minced onion
1 teaspoon minced garlic
2 cans (6 ounces each) chunk light tuna packed in water, drained
1 can (28 ounces) diced tomatoes
1 can (8 ounces) tomato sauce
24 pitted kalamata or black olives
2 tablespoons capers, drained

**For a mildly spicy dish, use ¼ teaspoon red pepper flakes. For a very spicy dish, use 1 teaspoon red pepper flakes.*

1. Cook pasta according to package directions; drain and return to saucepan. Add 1 teaspoon oil; toss to coat. Keep warm.

2. Heat remaining 3 tablespoons oil in large skillet over medium-high heat. Add red pepper flakes; cook and stir until sizzling. Add onion and garlic; cook and stir 1 minute. Add tuna; cook and stir 2 to 3 minutes. Add tomatoes, tomato sauce, olives and capers; cook until sauce is heated through, stirring frequently.

3. Add sauce to pasta; toss to coat. Serve immediately.

Makes 6 to 8 servings

SPICY MANICOTTI

3 cups ricotta cheese
1 cup grated Parmesan cheese, divided
2 eggs, lightly beaten
2½ tablespoons chopped fresh parsley
1 teaspoon Italian seasoning
½ teaspoon garlic powder
½ teaspoon salt
½ teaspoon black pepper
1 pound spicy Italian sausage
1 can (28 ounces) crushed tomatoes in purée
1 jar (26 ounces) marinara sauce
8 ounces uncooked manicotti shells

1. Preheat oven to 375°F. Grease 13×9-inch baking dish.

2. Combine ricotta, ¾ cup Parmesan, eggs, parsley, Italian seasoning, garlic powder, salt and pepper in medium bowl.

3. Crumble sausage into large skillet; brown over medium-high heat until no longer pink, stirring to separate meat. Drain sausage on paper towels; drain fat from skillet.

4. Add tomatoes and marinara sauce to same skillet; bring to a boil over high heat. Reduce heat to low; simmer, uncovered, 10 minutes. Pour about one third of sauce into prepared baking dish.

5. Stuff each shell with about ½ cup cheese mixture. Place in dish. Top shells with sausage and remaining sauce. Cover tightly with foil.

6. Bake 50 minutes to 1 hour or until pasta is tender. Let stand 5 minutes before serving. Sprinkle with remaining ¼ cup Parmesan. *Makes 8 servings*

PASTA PRIMAVERA

½ cup broccoli florets
½ cup cauliflower florets
1 carrot, peeled and thinly sliced
2 tablespoons olive oil
½ cup thinly sliced red bell pepper
½ cup thinly sliced yellow bell pepper
½ cup snow peas
½ cup sliced shiitake, morel or chanterelle mushrooms
1 clove garlic, minced
16 ounces uncooked linguine, cooked and drained
4 fresh basil leaves, minced

1. Steam broccoli, cauliflower and carrot 3 minutes or until crisp-tender.

2. Heat oil in large skillet over medium heat. Add steamed vegetables, bell peppers, snow peas, mushrooms and garlic; cook and stir 3 to 5 minutes.

3. Toss vegetables with hot pasta. Sprinkle with basil; serve immediately.

Makes 4 servings

Tip Shiitake are wild mushrooms with brown caps, a firm texture and thin tough stems, which should be trimmed away. Wipe mushrooms with a damp paper towel, brush with a mushroom brush or rinse briefly under cold running water to remove the dirt. (Do not soak in water.) Pat dry before using.

LINGUINE WITH CLAM SAUCE

- **8 ounces uncooked linguine**
- **2 tablespoons olive oil**
- **1 cup chopped onion**
- **1 can (about 14 ounces) stewed Italian-style tomatoes, drained and chopped**
- **2 cloves garlic, minced**
- **2 teaspoons dried basil**
- **½ cup dry white wine or chicken broth**
- **1 can (10 ounces) whole baby clams, drained, juice reserved**
- **⅓ cup chopped fresh parsley**
- **¼ teaspoon salt**
- **¼ teaspoon black pepper**

1. Cook pasta according to package directions; drain.

2. Heat oil in large skillet over medium heat. Add onion; cook and stir 3 minutes. Add tomatoes, garlic and basil; cook and stir 3 minutes. Stir in wine and reserved clam juice; bring to a boil and simmer, uncovered, 5 minutes.

3. Stir in clams, parsley, salt and pepper; cook 1 to 2 minutes or until heated through. Spoon over pasta. Serve immediately. *Makes 4 servings*

PASTA WITH CREAMY VODKA SAUCE

6 ounces uncooked campanelle or farfalle pasta
1 tablespoon unsalted butter
3 plum tomatoes, seeded and chopped
2 cloves garlic, minced
3 tablespoons vodka
½ cup whipping cream
¼ teaspoon salt
¼ teaspoon red pepper flakes
⅓ cup grated Parmesan cheese
2 tablespoons snipped fresh chives

1. Cook pasta according to package directions; drain and keep warm in saucepan.

2. Melt butter in large skillet over medium heat. Add tomatoes and garlic; cook 3 minutes, stirring frequently. Add vodka; simmer 2 minutes or until most of liquid has evaporated.

3. Stir in cream, salt and red pepper flakes; simmer 2 to 3 minutes or until slightly thickened. Remove from heat; let stand 2 minutes. Stir in Parmesan until melted.

4. Add sauce and chives to pasta; toss to coat. Serve immediately.

Makes 4 servings

SPAGHETTI ALLA BOLOGNESE

- 2 tablespoons olive oil
- 1 pound ground beef
- 1 medium onion, chopped
- ½ small carrot, finely chopped
- ½ stalk celery, finely chopped
- 1 cup dry white wine
- ½ cup milk
- ⅛ teaspoon ground nutmeg
- 1 can (about 14 ounces) whole peeled tomatoes, coarsely chopped, juice reserved
- 1 cup beef broth
- 3 tablespoons tomato paste
- 1 teaspoon salt
- 1 teaspoon dried basil
- ½ teaspoon dried thyme
- ⅛ teaspoon black pepper
- 1 bay leaf
- 16 ounces uncooked spaghetti
- 1 cup grated Parmesan cheese

1. Heat oil in large saucepan over medium heat. Add beef; cook 6 to 8 minutes, stirring to break up meat. Drain fat.

2. Add onion, carrot and celery; cook and stir 2 minutes. Stir in wine; cook 4 to 6 minutes or until wine has evaporated. Stir in milk and nutmeg; cook 3 to 4 minutes or until milk has almost evaporated. Remove from heat.

3. Press tomatoes with reserved juice through sieve into meat mixture; discard seeds.

4. Stir in broth, tomato paste, salt, basil, thyme, pepper and bay leaf; bring to a boil over medium-high heat. Reduce heat to medium-low; simmer 1 to 1½ hours or until most of liquid has evaporated and sauce thickens, stirring frequently. Discard bay leaf.

5. Cook pasta according to package directions; drain. Combine pasta and sauce in large bowl; toss gently to coat. Sprinkle with Parmesan.

Makes 4 to 6 servings

CLASSIC PESTO WITH LINGUINE

12 ounces uncooked linguine
2 tablespoons butter
¼ cup plus 1 tablespoon olive oil, divided
2 tablespoons pine nuts
1 cup tightly packed fresh basil leaves
2 cloves garlic
¼ teaspoon salt
¼ cup grated Parmesan cheese
1½ tablespoons grated Romano cheese

1. Cook pasta according to package directions; drain. Toss with butter in large serving bowl; keep warm.

2. Heat 1 tablespoon oil in small skillet over medium-low heat. Add pine nuts; cook and stir 30 to 45 seconds until light brown, shaking pan constantly. Remove with slotted spoon; drain on paper towels.

3. Place toasted pine nuts, basil, garlic and salt in food processor or blender. With motor running, add remaining ¼ cup oil in slow steady stream; process until blended and pine nuts are finely chopped.

4. Transfer basil mixture to small bowl. Stir in Parmesan and Romano.*

5. Add pesto sauce to pasta; toss well to coat. Serve immediately.

Makes 4 servings

**Pesto sauce can be stored at this point in airtight container; pour thin layer of olive oil over pesto and cover. Refrigerate up to 1 week. Bring to room temperature before using. Proceed as directed in step 5.*

CHICKEN TETRAZZINI WITH ROASTED RED PEPPERS

6 ounces uncooked egg noodles
3 tablespoons butter
¼ cup all-purpose flour
1 can (about 14 ounces) chicken broth
1 cup whipping cream
2 tablespoons dry sherry
2 cans (6 ounces each) sliced mushrooms, drained
1 jar (about 7 ounces) roasted red peppers, drained and cut into ½-inch strips
2 cups chopped cooked chicken
1 teaspoon Italian seasoning
½ cup grated Parmesan cheese

1. Cook noodles according to package directions; drain and keep warm.

2. Melt butter in medium saucepan over medium heat. Add flour and whisk until smooth. Gradually whisk in broth; bring to a boil over high heat. Remove from heat; stir in cream and sherry until well blended.

3. Combine mushrooms, roasted peppers and noodles in large bowl; toss well. Stir in half of sauce. Combine remaining sauce, chicken and Italian seasoning in medium bowl.

4. Spoon noodle mixture onto serving plates; top with chicken mixture. Sprinkle with Parmesan.

Makes 6 servings

FETTUCCINE ALLA CARBONARA

12 ounces uncooked fettuccine
4 ounces pancetta or bacon, cut crosswise into ½-inch pieces
3 cloves garlic, cut into halves
¼ cup dry white wine
⅓ cup whipping cream
1 egg
1 egg yolk
⅔ cup grated Parmesan cheese, divided
Dash white pepper

1. Cook pasta according to package directions; drain and keep warm in saucepan.

2. Cook and stir pancetta and garlic in large skillet over medium-low heat 4 minutes or until lightly browned. Drain and discard all but 2 tablespoons drippings from skillet.

3. Add wine to skillet; cook over medium heat 3 minutes or until wine is almost evaporated. Add cream; cook and stir 2 minutes. Remove from heat. Discard garlic.

4. Whisk egg and egg yolk in top of double boiler; place over simmering water, adjusting heat to maintain simmer. Whisk ⅓ cup Parmesan and pepper into egg mixture; cook and stir until thickened.

5. Pour pancetta mixture over pasta; toss to coat. Cook over medium-low heat until heated through. Add egg mixture; toss to coat. Serve with remaining ⅓ cup Parmesan. *Makes 4 servings*

Modern Pasta

SUMMER SPAGHETTI

1 pound plum tomatoes, coarsely chopped
1 medium onion, chopped
6 pitted green olives, chopped
⅓ cup chopped fresh parsley
2 tablespoons finely shredded fresh basil *or* ¾ teaspoon dried basil
2 cloves garlic, minced
2 teaspoons drained capers
½ teaspoon paprika
¼ teaspoon dried oregano
1 tablespoon red wine vinegar
½ cup olive oil
16 ounces uncooked spaghetti

1. Combine tomatoes, onion, olives, parsley, basil, garlic, capers, paprika and oregano in medium bowl; mix well. Drizzle with vinegar. Add oil; stir until well blended. Cover and refrigerate at least 6 hours or overnight.

2. Cook pasta according to package directions; drain. Toss hot pasta with tomato mixture.

Makes 4 to 6 servings

SCALLOPS VERMICELLI WITH CAPERS

4 ounces uncooked whole wheat vermicelli or thin spaghetti
½ cup grape tomatoes, halved
¼ cup finely chopped green bell pepper
¼ cup dry white wine
3 tablespoons capers, rinsed and drained
3 tablespoons extra virgin olive oil, divided
2 teaspoons dried oregano
½ teaspoon paprika
¼ teaspoon salt
¼ teaspoon black pepper
1 pound sea scallops, rinsed and patted dry

1. Cook pasta according to package directions; drain. Place in large bowl and keep warm.

2. Combine tomatoes, bell pepper, wine, capers, 2 tablespoons oil, oregano, paprika, salt and black pepper in medium bowl.

3. Heat remaining 1 tablespoon oil in large nonstick skillet over medium-high heat. Cook scallops in batches 2 minutes per side. Add to pasta; keep warm.

4. Add tomato mixture to skillet; cook and stir 1 minute. Pour over pasta and scallops; toss to coat. *Makes 2 servings*

RAVIOLI PANZANELLA SALAD

1 package (9 ounces) refrigerated cheese ravioli or tortellini
2 tablespoons olive oil
2 teaspoons white wine vinegar
⅛ teaspoon black pepper
1 cup halved grape tomatoes *or* 1 chopped tomato
½ cup sliced pimiento-stuffed olives
¼ cup finely chopped celery
1 shallot, finely chopped *or* ¼ cup finely chopped red onion
¼ cup chopped fresh Italian parsley

1. Cook pasta according to package directions; drain. Place in large bowl; let stand 10 minutes.

2. Whisk oil, vinegar and pepper in small bowl until well blended; pour over ravioli. Add tomatoes, olives, celery and shallot; toss gently. Sprinkle with parsley. *Makes 4 to 6 servings*

PASTA WITH SPINACH & RICOTTA

8 ounces uncooked tri-colored rotini pasta
2 teaspoons olive oil
1 package (10 ounces) frozen chopped spinach, thawed and squeezed dry
2 teaspoons minced garlic
1 cup ricotta cheese
½ cup water
¼ cup grated Parmesan cheese, divided
Salt and black pepper

1. Cook pasta according to package directions; drain and keep warm.

2. Heat oil in large skillet over medium-low heat. Add spinach and garlic; cook and stir 5 minutes. Stir in ricotta, water and 2 tablespoons Parmesan. Season with salt and pepper.

3. Add pasta to skillet; stir until well blended. Sprinkle with remaining 2 tablespoons Parmesan. *Makes 4 servings*

LINGUINE WITH CLAMS & MARINARA SAUCE

1⅓ cups Marinara Sauce (recipe follows)
8 ounces uncooked linguine
1 teaspoon olive oil
¼ cup chopped shallots
3 cloves garlic, finely chopped
2 cans (6 ounces each) minced clams
2 tablespoons pesto sauce
¼ teaspoon red pepper flakes
¼ cup chopped fresh parsley

1. Prepare Marinara Sauce. Cook pasta according to package directions; drain and return to saucepan.

2. Heat oil in large nonstick saucepan over medium heat until hot. Add shallots and garlic; cover and cook 2 minutes.

3. Drain clams, reserving ½ cup juice. Add clams, reserved juice, Marinara Sauce, pesto and red pepper flakes to saucepan; cook 10 minutes, stirring occasionally.

4. Pour sauce over pasta; toss to coat. Sprinkle with parsley.

Makes 4 servings

MARINARA SAUCE

1½ tablespoons olive oil
3 cloves garlic, minced
1 can (28 ounces) Italian plum tomatoes, undrained
¼ cup tomato paste
2 teaspoons dried basil
½ teaspoon sugar
½ teaspoon salt
¼ teaspoon red pepper flakes

Heat oil in large skillet over medium heat. Add garlic; cook and stir 3 minutes. Stir in remaining ingredients; bring to a boil. Reduce heat to low; simmer, uncovered, 10 minutes.

Makes about 3½ cups

WHOLE WHEAT SPAGHETTI WITH CAULIFLOWER & FETA

3 tablespoons olive oil
1 onion, chopped
4 cloves garlic, minced
1 head cauliflower, cut into bite-size florets
⅔ cup white wine or water
1 teaspoon salt
½ teaspoon black pepper
8 ounces uncooked whole wheat spaghetti
1 pint grape tomatoes, cut in half
½ cup coarsely chopped walnuts
¼ teaspoon red pepper flakes (optional)
½ cup crumbled feta cheese

1. Heat oil in large skillet over medium heat. Add onion; cook and stir 3 minutes or until soft. Add garlic; cook and stir 2 minutes. Add cauliflower; cook and stir 5 minutes. Add wine, salt and pepper; cover and cook about 15 minutes or until cauliflower is crisp-tender.

2. Cook pasta according to package directions. Reserve ½ cup pasta cooking water; drain pasta and keep warm.

3. Add tomatoes, walnuts, red pepper flakes, if desired, and reserved pasta water to skillet; cook 2 to 3 minutes or until tomatoes begin to soften.

4. Toss pasta with cauliflower mixture in skillet or serving bowl; top with feta.

Makes 4 servings

PESTO PASTA WITH ASPARAGUS & TOMATOES

8 ounces uncooked thin spaghetti
8 ounces asparagus spears, cut into 2-inch pieces
1 jar (3½ ounces) pesto sauce
1 medium tomato, chopped
2 tablespoons olive oil
1 clove garlic, minced
½ teaspoon black pepper
¼ cup grated Parmesan cheese

1. Cook pasta according to package directions, adding asparagus during last 3 minutes of cooking.

2. Combine pesto, tomato, oil, garlic and pepper in medium bowl; stir until well blended.

3. Drain pasta and asparagus; place in large bowl. Add pesto mixture; toss gently to coat. Sprinkle with Parmesan. *Makes 4 servings*

Tip Select asparagus with firm, smooth green stems and tightly closed tips; tips that are open are a sign of age. Avoid wilted spears and asparagus that has a strong odor. The best storage method is to keep asparagus upright with the stems in several inches of water. Or wrap the bunch in damp paper towels and place in a plastic bag. Since it loses its natural sugar during storage, asparagus should be refrigerated as quickly as possible and used within a day or two for best flavor.

PASTA WITH ONIONS & GOAT CHEESE

- 1 tablespoon olive oil
- 3 to 4 cups thinly sliced sweet onions
- ¾ cup (3 ounces) crumbled goat cheese
- ¼ cup milk
- 6 ounces uncooked campanelle or farfalle pasta
- 1 clove garlic, minced
- 2 tablespoons dry white wine or vegetable broth
- 1½ teaspoons chopped fresh sage *or* ½ teaspoon dried sage
- ½ teaspoon salt
- ¼ teaspoon black pepper
- 2 tablespoons chopped toasted walnuts

1. Heat oil in large nonstick skillet over medium heat. Add onions; cook 20 to 25 minutes or until golden and caramelized, stirring occasionally.

2. Combine goat cheese and milk in small bowl; stir until well blended.

3. Cook pasta according to package directions; drain and keep warm.

4. Add garlic to onions in skillet; cook about 3 minutes or until softened. Add wine, sage, salt and pepper; cook until liquid has evaporated. Remove from heat. Add pasta and goat cheese mixture; stir until cheese is melted. Sprinkle with walnuts.

Makes 4 servings

THREE–PEPPER FETTUCCINE

- **1 *each* roasted red bell pepper, yellow bell pepper and jalapeño pepper (see Tip)**
- **1 tablespoon olive oil**
- **½ teaspoon chopped fresh thyme *or* ¼ teaspoon dried thyme**
- **½ teaspoon salt**
- **¼ teaspoon black pepper**
- **1 package (9 ounces) refrigerated fresh fettuccine**
- **3 ounces mild goat cheese, crumbled**
- **2 tablespoons minced chives or green onions**

1. Core and seed bell peppers; cut into thin strips and place in large bowl. Core, seed and mince jalapeño; add to bell peppers. Stir in oil, thyme, salt and black pepper.

2. Cook pasta according to package directions; drain. Add pasta to pepper mixture; toss gently to coat. Add goat cheese; toss again. Sprinkle with chives.

Makes 4 to 6 servings

Tip: To roast peppers, broil on foil-lined baking sheet or broiler pan, turning occasionally, until peppers are charred all over. Place peppers in a bowl and cover with plastic wrap, or place charred peppers in a brown paper bag and close bag. Let steam at least 10 minutes. Remove charred skin. Proceed with recipe. If desired, peppers can be roasted in advance and refrigerated.

GEMELLI & GRILLED SUMMER VEGETABLES

2 large bell peppers (red and yellow)
12 stalks asparagus, trimmed
2 slices red onion
3 tablespoons plus 1 teaspoon olive oil, divided
8 ounces uncooked gemelli or rotini pasta
2 tablespoons pine nuts
1 clove garlic
1 cup loosely packed fresh basil leaves
¼ cup grated Parmesan cheese
¼ teaspoon salt
¼ teaspoon black pepper
1 cup grape or cherry tomatoes

1. Prepare grill for direct cooking. Cut bell peppers in half; remove and discard seeds. Grill bell peppers, skin side down, on covered grill over medium heat 10 to 12 minutes or until skins are blackened. Place peppers in paper or plastic bag; let stand 15 minutes. Remove and discard blackened skins. Cut peppers into large pieces. Place in large bowl.

2. Toss asparagus and onion with 1 teaspoon oil in medium bowl. Grill, covered, over medium heat 8 to 10 minutes or until tender, turning once. Cut asparagus into 2-inch pieces and coarsely chop onion; add asparagus and onion to bell peppers.

3. Cook pasta according to package directions; drain well and add to vegetables.

4. Combine pine nuts and garlic in food processor; process until coarsely chopped. Add basil; process until finely chopped. With motor running, add remaining 3 tablespoons oil; process until blended. Stir in Parmesan, salt and pepper. Add basil mixture and tomatoes to pasta and vegetables; toss to coat. Serve immediately.

Makes 4 servings

Pasta al Forno

BAKED GNOCCHI

1 package (about 17 ounces) gnocchi
⅓ cup olive oil
3 cloves garlic, minced
1 package (10 ounces) frozen spinach, thawed and squeezed dry
1 can (about 14 ounces) diced tomatoes
1 teaspoon Italian seasoning
Salt and black pepper
½ cup grated Parmesan cheese
½ cup (2 ounces) shredded mozzarella cheese

1. Preheat oven to 350°F. Grease 2½-quart casserole or gratin dish.

2. Cook gnocchi according to package directions; drain and keep warm.

3. Heat oil in large saucepan or Dutch oven over medium heat. Add garlic; cook and stir 30 seconds. Stir in spinach; cover and cook 2 minutes. Add tomatoes, Italian seasoning, salt and pepper; cook and stir about 5 minutes. Gently stir in gnocchi.

4. Transfer gnocchi mixture to prepared casserole. Sprinkle with Parmesan and mozzarella.

5. Bake 20 to 30 minutes or until casserole is bubbly and cheese is melted.

Makes 4 to 6 servings

EASY CHEESY LASAGNA

- **2 tablespoons olive oil**
- **3 small zucchini, quartered and thinly sliced**
- **1 package (8 ounces) mushrooms, thinly sliced**
- **1 medium onion, chopped**
- **5 cloves garlic, minced**
- **2 containers (15 ounces each) ricotta cheese**
- **2 eggs**
- **¼ cup grated Parmesan cheese**
- **1 teaspoon salt**
- **½ teaspoon Italian seasoning**
- **⅛ teaspoon black pepper**
- **1 can (28 ounces) crushed tomatoes in purée**
- **1 jar (26 ounces) spaghetti sauce**
- **16 ounces uncooked lasagna noodles**
- **4 cups (16 ounces) shredded mozzarella cheese, divided**

1. Preheat oven to 375°F. Grease 13×9-inch baking dish or lasagna pan.

2. Heat oil in large skillet over medium heat. Add zucchini, mushrooms, onion and garlic; cook and stir 5 minutes or until vegetables are tender.

3. Combine ricotta, eggs, Parmesan, salt, Italian seasoning and pepper in medium bowl; mix well. Combine tomatoes and spaghetti sauce in large bowl.

4. Spread about ¾ cup tomato mixture in prepared baking dish. Top with layer of noodles, overlapping noodles. Spread half of vegetable mixture over noodles; top with half of ricotta mixture. Sprinkle with 1 cup mozzarella. Top with second layer of noodles, 1 cup tomato mixture and remaining vegetable and ricotta cheese mixtures. Sprinkle with 1 cup mozzarella. Place third layer of noodles over mozzarella; top with remaining tomato mixture and 2 cups mozzarella. Cover dish tightly with foil.

5. Bake 1 hour or until noodles in center are soft. Uncover and bake 5 minutes or until cheese is melted and lightly browned. Let stand, covered, 15 minutes before serving.

Makes 6 servings

BAKED RAVIOLI WITH PUMPKIN SAUCE

1 package (9 ounces) refrigerated cheese ravioli
1 tablespoon butter
1 shallot, finely chopped
1 cup whipping cream
1 cup canned solid-pack pumpkin
½ cup shredded Asiago cheese, divided
½ teaspoon salt
¼ teaspoon ground nutmeg
⅛ teaspoon black pepper
½ cup coarse plain dry bread crumbs or small croutons

1. Preheat oven to 350°F. Grease 2-quart baking dish.

2. Cook ravioli according to package directions; drain and keep warm.

3. Melt butter in medium saucepan over medium heat. Add shallot; cook and stir 3 minutes or until tender. Add cream, pumpkin, ¼ cup Asiago, salt, nutmeg and pepper; cook and stir over low heat 2 minutes or until cheese melts. Gently stir in ravioli.

4. Transfer ravioli mixture to prepared baking dish. Combine remaining ¼ cup Asiago and bread crumbs in small bowl; sprinkle over ravioli.

5. Bake 15 minutes or until heated through and topping is lightly browned.

Makes 4 servings

SPINACH STUFFED MANICOTTI

8 uncooked manicotti shells
2 teaspoons olive oil
1 teaspoon minced garlic
1 teaspoon dried rosemary
1 teaspoon dried sage
1 teaspoon dried oregano
1 teaspoon dried thyme
1½ cups chopped fresh tomatoes
1 package (10 ounces) frozen chopped spinach, thawed and squeezed dry
½ cup ricotta cheese
½ cup fresh whole wheat bread crumbs
2 egg whites, lightly beaten

1. Cook pasta according to package directions; drain. Rinse under cold running water until cool enough to handle.

2. Preheat oven to 350°F. Heat oil in medium saucepan over medium heat. Add garlic, rosemary, sage, oregano and thyme; cook and stir about 1 minute. Stir in tomatoes; simmer 10 minutes over low heat, stirring occasionally.

3. Combine spinach, ricotta and bread crumbs in medium bowl; mix well. Fold in egg whites. Fill manicotti shells with spinach mixture.

4. Spread one third of tomato sauce in bottom of 13×9-inch baking dish. Arrange manicotti in dish; pour remaining tomato sauce over top. Cover with foil.

5. Bake 30 minutes or until hot and bubbly.

Makes 4 servings

SHELLS & FONTINA

- **8 ounces uncooked small whole wheat shell pasta**
- **1¾ cups milk**
- **4 large fresh sage leaves *or* ½ teaspoon dried sage**
- **4 tablespoons butter**
- **4 tablespoons flour**
- **½ cup tomato sauce**
- **Salt and black pepper**
- **¾ cup grated Parmesan cheese, divided**
- **5½ ounces fontina cheese, shredded***
- **¼ cup dry bread crumbs**

**It is easier to shred fontina cheese if it is very cold. Keep it in the refrigerator or place it in the freezer 10 minutes before shredding.*

1. Preheat oven to 350°F. Cook pasta according to package directions until barely al dente. Drain; rinse under cold running water to stop cooking.

2. Meanwhile, heat milk with sage leaves in small saucepan over medium heat; do not boil. Melt butter in large saucepan over medium-low heat until bubbly. Whisk in flour until smooth paste forms; cook and stir 2 minutes without browning.

3. Remove sage leaves and gradually whisk milk into butter mixture over medium heat. Cook 4 to 5 minutes, whisking constantly, until mixture begins to bubble and thickens slightly. Stir in tomato sauce and season with salt and pepper. Remove from heat; stir in ½ cup Parmesan until smooth.

4. Add pasta to sauce; stir to coat. Spoon one third of pasta mixture into 2-quart casserole; top with one third of shredded fontina. Repeat layers twice. Sprinkle with bread crumbs and remaining ¼ cup Parmesan.

5. Bake 20 to 25 minutes or until hot and bubbly. *Makes 4 to 6 servings*

PESTO LASAGNA

16 ounces uncooked lasagna noodles
3 tablespoons olive oil
1½ cups chopped onions
3 cloves garlic, finely chopped
3 packages (10 ounces each) frozen chopped spinach, thawed and squeezed dry
Salt and black pepper
3 cups (24 ounces) ricotta cheese
1½ cups pesto sauce
¾ cup grated Parmesan cheese
½ cup pine nuts, toasted*
4 cups (16 ounces) shredded mozzarella cheese

**To toast pine nuts, spread in single layer in heavy skillet. Cook and stir over medium heat 1 to 2 minutes, stirring frequently, until nuts are lightly browned. Immediately remove from skillet.*

1. Preheat oven to 350°F. Grease 13×9-inch baking dish or lasagna pan. Partially cook lasagna noodles according to package directions.

2. Heat oil in large skillet over medium-high heat. Add onions and garlic; cook and stir until translucent. Add spinach; cook and stir about 5 minutes. Season with salt and pepper. Transfer to large bowl.

3. Add ricotta, pesto, Parmesan and pine nuts to spinach mixture; mix well.

4. Layer 5 lasagna noodles, slightly overlapping, in prepared baking dish. Top with one third of ricotta mixture and one third of mozzarella. Repeat layers twice.

5. Bake about 35 minutes or until hot and bubbly. *Makes 8 servings*

TUSCAN BAKED RIGATONI

- **1 pound bulk Italian sausage**
- **16 ounces uncooked rigatoni pasta, cooked, drained and kept warm**
- **2 cups (8 ounces) shredded fontina cheese**
- **2 tablespoons olive oil**
- **2 bulbs fennel, thinly sliced**
- **4 cloves garlic, minced**
- **1 can (28 ounces) crushed tomatoes**
- **1 cup whipping cream**
- **1 teaspoon salt**
- **1 teaspoon black pepper**
- **8 cups packed torn stemmed spinach**
- **1 can (about 15 ounces) cannellini beans, rinsed and drained**
- **2 tablespoons pine nuts**
- **½ cup grated Parmesan cheese**

1. Preheat oven to 350°F. Grease 4-quart casserole.

2. Brown sausage in large skillet over medium-high heat, stirring to break up meat. Drain fat. Transfer sausage to large bowl. Add pasta and fontina; mix well.

3. Heat oil in same skillet over medium heat. Add fennel and garlic; cook and stir 3 minutes or until fennel is tender. Add tomatoes, cream, salt and pepper; cook and stir until slightly thickened. Stir in spinach, beans and pine nuts; cook until heated through.

4. Pour sauce mixture over pasta mixture; toss to coat. Transfer to prepared casserole; sprinkle evenly with Parmesan.

5. Bake 30 minutes or until hot and bubbly.

Makes 6 to 8 servings

MANICOTTI

- **1 container (15 ounces) ricotta cheese**
- **2 cups (8 ounces) shredded mozzarella cheese**
- **½ cup cottage cheese**
- **2 eggs, beaten**
- **2 tablespoons grated Parmesan cheese**
- **½ teaspoon minced garlic**
- **Salt and black pepper**
- **8 ounces uncooked manicotti shells**
- **1 pound ground beef**
- **1 jar (about 26 ounces) pasta sauce**
- **2 cups water**

1. Preheat oven to 375°F.

2. Combine ricotta, mozzarella, cottage cheese, eggs, Parmesan, garlic, salt and pepper in large bowl; mix well. Fill manicotti shells with cheese mixture; place in 13×9-inch baking dish.

3. Brown beef in large skillet over medium-high heat 6 to 8 minutes, stirring to break up meat. Drain fat. Stir in pasta sauce and water (mixture will be thin). Pour sauce over filled manicotti shells. Cover dish with foil.

4. Bake 1 hour or until sauce is thickened and shells are tender.

Makes 6 servings

CREAMY PUMPKIN BAKED PENNE

14 to 16 ounces uncooked multigrain or whole wheat penne pasta
2 teaspoons olive oil
1 small onion, chopped
3 cloves garlic, minced
1 can (28 ounces) crushed tomatoes
1 can (15 ounces) solid-pack pumpkin
¾ cup ricotta cheese
½ cup vegetable or chicken broth
1 tablespoon Italian seasoning
¾ teaspoon red pepper flakes
1 cup (4 ounces) shredded mozzarella cheese
⅓ cup grated Parmesan cheese

1. Preheat oven to 375°F. Grease 13×9-inch baking dish. Cook pasta according to package directions until barely al dente; drain.

2. Heat oil in large saucepan or Dutch oven over medium heat. Add onion and garlic; cook and stir 3 minutes. Stir in tomatoes, pumpkin, ricotta, broth, Italian seasoning and red pepper flakes. Reduce heat to medium-low; simmer 5 minutes. Add pasta; toss to coat.

3. Transfer pasta mixture to prepared baking dish; sprinkle with mozzarella and Parmesan.

4. Bake 30 to 35 minutes or until cheeses are golden brown.

Makes 6 to 8 servings

BAKED PASTA WITH RICOTTA

- **16 ounces uncooked rigatoni or penne pasta**
- **1 container (15 ounces) ricotta cheese**
- **⅔ cup grated Parmesan cheese**
- **2 eggs, lightly beaten**
- **½ teaspoon salt**
- **⅛ teaspoon black pepper**
- **2 jars (26 ounces each) marinara sauce**
- **3 cups (12 ounces) shredded mozzarella cheese**

1. Preheat oven to 375°F. Grease 13×9-inch baking dish.

2. Cook rigatoni according to package directions; drain. Beat ricotta, Parmesan, eggs, salt and pepper in medium bowl until well blended.

3. Spread 2 cups marinara sauce over bottom of prepared baking dish; spoon half of cooked pasta over sauce. Top with half of ricotta mixture and 1 cup mozzarella. Repeat layers of marinara sauce, pasta and ricotta mixture. Top with 1 cup mozzarella, remaining marinara sauce and 1 cup mozzarella. Cover with foil.

4. Bake about 1 hour or until bubbly. Uncover and bake about 5 minutes or until cheese is completely melted. Let stand 15 minutes before serving.

Makes 12 servings

Risotto Magnifico

GOLDEN RISOTTO WITH TURKEY & ASPARAGUS

½ cup minced onion
1 tablespoon butter
1 tablespoon CARAPELLI® olive oil
1 cup arborio or California medium-grain rice
1 pinch saffron threads
4½ cups hot chicken broth
1 pound asparagus, green beans or peas cut into 1-inch lengths, blanched
1 package JENNIE-O TURKEY STORE® Smoked Turkey Sausage or Turkey Breast, cut into 1-inch diagonal slices
½ cup grated Parmesan cheese
Chopped chives

In large saucepan, sauté onion in butter and olive oil 2 minutes or until tender. Stir in rice until evenly coated. Add saffron to broth. Add 1 cup broth to rice. Stir until liquid is absorbed. Continue to add broth, 1 cup at a time, until all liquid is absorbed, about 10 minutes. Stir in asparagus, turkey sausage and cheese. Sprinkle with chopped chives. *Makes 4 servings*

Prep Time: 15 minutes **Cook Time:** 15 minutes

ORZO RISOTTO WITH SHRIMP & VEGETABLES

- 2 teaspoons olive oil
- 1 zucchini, halved and sliced
- 2 teaspoons grated lemon peel
- 1 cup sliced mushrooms
- ½ cup chopped onion
- 2 cloves garlic
- ¾ teaspoon dried sage
- ¼ to ½ teaspoon dried thyme
- 1¼ cups uncooked orzo pasta
- 2 cans (about 14 ounces each) chicken broth
- 8 ounces shrimp, peeled and deveined
- ¾ cup frozen peas, thawed
- ¼ cup grated Parmesan cheese
- Salt and black pepper

1. Heat oil in large saucepan over medium heat. Add zucchini and lemon peel; cook and stir 2 to 3 minutes or until zucchini is tender. Remove from saucepan; set aside.

2. Add mushrooms, onion, garlic, sage and thyme to saucepan; cook and stir 2 to 3 minutes or until onion is tender. Stir in orzo; cook and stir until lightly browned.

3. Bring broth to a boil in medium saucepan. Add broth to orzo mixture, ½ cup at a time, stirring constantly until broth is absorbed before adding next ½ cup. Continue adding broth and stirring until orzo is tender. (Total cooking time will be 15 to 20 minutes.)

4. Stir shrimp and peas into orzo mixture during last half of cooking time. Stir in zucchini mixture during last 2 to 3 minutes of cooking time. Stir in Parmesan; season with salt and pepper. *Makes 4 servings*

CHICKEN MUSHROOM RISOTTO

3 skinless, boneless chicken breast halves (about ¾ pound), cut into cubes
1 small onion, finely chopped (about ¼ cup)
1 small carrot, chopped (about ¼ cup)
1 cup uncooked regular long-grain white rice
1 can (10¾ ounces) CAMPBELL'S® Healthy Request® Condensed Cream of Mushroom Soup
1¾ cups SWANSON® Chicken Stock
⅛ teaspoon ground black pepper
½ cup frozen peas

1. Cook the chicken in a 10-inch nonstick skillet over medium-high heat until well browned, stirring often. Remove the chicken from the skillet.

2. Stir the onion, carrot and rice in the skillet and cook and stir until the rice is browned.

3. Stir in the soup, stock and black pepper and heat to a boil. Reduce the heat to low. Cover and cook for 15 minutes.

4. Stir in the peas. Return the chicken to the skillet. Cover and cook for 5 minutes or until the chicken is cooked through and the rice is tender.

Makes 4 servings

Prep Time: 15 minutes **Cook Time:** 35 minutes
Total Time: 50 minutes

SAUSAGE & RED PEPPER RISOTTO

- 4½ cups chicken broth
- 8 ounces sweet Italian sausage links, removed from casing
- 1 tablespoon olive oil
- 1 large onion, chopped
- 1 medium red bell pepper, chopped
- 1 clove garlic, finely chopped
- 1½ cups arborio or regular rice
- ⅓ cup dry white wine or chicken broth
- ⅛ teaspoon dried oregano leaves, crushed
- 1 cup RAGÚ® Old World Style® Pasta Sauce or RAGÚ® Light Pasta Sauce
- ¼ cup grated Parmesan cheese
- ⅛ teaspoon ground black pepper

1. Heat chicken broth in 2-quart saucepan.

2. Brown sausage in heavy-duty 3-quart saucepan over medium-high heat 4 minutes or until sausage is brown. Remove sausage with slotted spoon and set aside.

3. In same 3-quart saucepan, add oil and cook onion over medium heat, stirring occasionally, 3 minutes. Stir in bell pepper and garlic and cook 1 minute. Add rice and cook, stirring occasionally, 1 minute. Slowly add 1 cup broth, wine and oregano and cook, stirring constantly, until liquid is absorbed. Continue adding 2 cups broth, 1 cup at a time, stirring frequently, until liquid is absorbed.

4. Meanwhile, stir Pasta Sauce into remaining 1½ cups broth; heat through. Continue adding broth mixture, 1 cup at a time, stirring frequently, until rice is slightly creamy and just tender. Return sausage to saucepan and stir in cheese and black pepper. Garnish, if desired, with additional fresh grated Parmesan cheese. Serve immediately. *Makes 4 servings*

Prep Time: 15 minutes ✦ **Cook Time:** 45 minutes

PEASANT RISOTTO

2 cans (about 14 ounces each) chicken broth
1 tablespoon olive oil
3 ounces chopped prosciutto or ham
2 cloves garlic, minced
1 can (about 15 ounces) Great Northern or cannellini beans, rinsed and drained
1 cup arborio or white short-grain rice
¼ cup chopped green onions
½ teaspoon dried sage
1½ cups packed Swiss chard, rinsed, stemmed and shredded
½ cup grated Parmesan cheese

1. Bring broth to a simmer in medium saucepan; keep warm over low heat.

2. Heat oil in large saucepan over medium heat. Add prosciutto and garlic; cook and stir until garlic is browned.

3. Add beans, rice, green onions and sage; cook and stir 2 minutes. Add warm broth; bring to a boil. Reduce heat to low; cook about 25 minutes or until rice is creamy, stirring frequently.

4. Stir in Swiss chard and Parmesan. Remove from heat; cover and let stand 2 minutes or until Swiss chard is wilted. Serve immediately.

Makes 4 servings

Tip One bunch of Swiss chard typically weighs just under 1 pound. For this recipe, you'll need ⅓ to ½ pound chard. If chard is not available, you can substitute fresh spinach.

CRAB AND ASPARAGUS RISOTTO

2 tablespoons olive oil
1 medium orange pepper, diced (about 1 cup)
½ cup chopped onion or shallots
2 cups uncooked Arborio rice or regular long-grain white rice
½ cup dry white wine
6 cups SWANSON® Chicken Broth (Regular, Natural Goodness® or Certified Organic)
½ pound asparagus or green beans
½ pound refrigerated pasteurized crabmeat (about 1½ cups)
¼ cup grated Parmesan cheese

1. Heat the oil in a 4-quart saucepan over medium heat. Add the pepper and onion and cook for 3 minutes or until the vegetables are tender.

2. Add the rice to the saucepan and cook and stir for 2 minutes. Add the wine and cook and stir until it's absorbed. Add **2 cups** of the broth and cook and stir until it's absorbed. Add the remaining broth, **½ cup** at a time, stirring until the broth is absorbed before adding more. Stir in the asparagus and crabmeat with the last broth addition.

3. Stir in the cheese. Remove the saucepan from the heat. Cover and let stand for 5 minutes. Serve the risotto with additional cheese, if desired.

Makes 8 servings

Kitchen Tip: If you have some light or heavy cream on hand, stir in **2 tablespoons** with the Parmesan cheese for a creamier dish.

Prep Time: 15 minutes ✦ **Cook Time:** 25 minutes ✦
Stand Time: 5 minutes

CHICKEN & VEGETABLE RISOTTO

6 cups chicken broth
1 tablespoon olive oil
2 cups sliced mushrooms
½ cup chopped onion (about 1 small)
4 cloves garlic, minced
1½ cups uncooked arborio rice
2 cups broccoli florets, cooked until crisp-tender
1 pound chicken tenders, cut into 1½-inch pieces, cooked
4 plum tomatoes, seeded and chopped
¼ cup finely chopped fresh parsley *or* 1 tablespoon dried parsley flakes
3 to 4 tablespoons finely chopped fresh basil *or* 1 tablespoon dried basil
½ teaspoon salt
½ teaspoon black pepper
2 tablespoons grated Parmesan or Romano cheese

1. Bring broth to a simmer in medium saucepan; keep warm over low heat.

2. Heat oil in large saucepan over medium heat. Add mushrooms, onion and garlic; cook and stir about 5 minutes or until tender.

3. Add rice; cook and stir 1 to 2 minutes. Add broth, ½ cup at a time, stirring constantly until broth is absorbed before adding next ½ cup. Continue adding broth and stirring until rice is tender and mixture is creamy. (Total cooking time will be 20 to 25 minutes.)

4. Add broccoli, chicken, tomatoes, parsley, basil, salt and pepper; cook and stir 2 to 3 minutes or until heated through. Sprinkle with Parmesan.

Makes 4 servings

EASY RISOTTO WITH BACON & PEAS

6 slices OSCAR MAYER® Bacon, cut into 1-inch pieces
1 medium onion, chopped (about 1 cup)
1½ cups medium grain rice, uncooked
2 cloves garlic, minced
3 cans (15 ounces each) chicken broth
4 ounces (½ of 8-ounce package) PHILADELPHIA® Cream Cheese, cubed
1 cup frozen peas, thawed
2 tablespoons chopped fresh parsley
2 tablespoons KRAFT® Grated Parmesan Cheese, divided

COOK bacon and onion in large skillet on medium-high heat 5 minutes or just until bacon is crisp, stirring occasionally.

ADD rice and garlic; cook 3 minutes or until rice is opaque, stirring frequently. Gradually add one-half can broth; cook and stir 3 minutes or until broth is completely absorbed. Repeat with remaining broth, adding cream cheese with last addition of broth and cooking 5 minutes or until cream cheese is completely melted and mixture is well blended.

STIR in peas; cook 2 minutes or until peas are heated through, stirring occasionally. Remove from heat. Stir in parsley and 1 tablespoon of Parmesan cheese. Serve topped with the remaining 1 tablespoon Parmesan cheese. *Makes 6 servings (1 cup each)*

Substitution: Prepare as directed, using fat-free reduced-sodium chicken broth.

Serving Suggestion: Serve with hot crusty bread and a mixed green salad topped with your favorite KRAFT® Dressing.

Prep Time: 10 minutes **Cook Time:** 30 minutes
Total Time: 40 minutes

Risotto with Vegetables

SUN-DRIED TOMATO RISOTTO

1 jar (8 ounces) oil-packed sun-dried tomatoes
1½ cups uncooked arborio rice or regular long-grain white rice
4 cups SWANSON® Chicken Broth (Regular, Natural Goodness® or Certified Organic), heated
1 cup frozen peas, thawed
¼ cup walnuts, toasted and chopped

1. Drain the tomatoes, reserving **2 tablespoons** oil. Chop enough tomatoes to make **½ cup**.

2. Heat the reserved oil in a 3-quart saucepan over medium heat. Add the tomatoes and rice and cook and stir for 2 minutes.

3. Add **1 cup** broth and cook and stir until it's absorbed. Add the remaining broth, **½ cup** at a time, stirring until it's absorbed before adding more. Stir in the peas and walnuts with the last broth addition.

4. Remove the saucepan from the heat. Cover and let stand for 5 minutes.

Makes 4 servings

Kitchen Tip: To quickly thaw the peas, place them in a colander and run under warm water.

Parmesan Sun-Dried Tomato Risotto: Substitute grated Parmesan cheese for the walnuts.

Prep Time: 5 minutes ✦ **Cook Time:** 25 minutes ✦
Stand Time: 5 minutes

SPINACH PARMESAN RISOTTO

3⅔ cups vegetable or chicken broth
½ teaspoon white pepper
2 teaspoons olive oil
1 cup uncooked arborio rice
1½ cups chopped fresh spinach
½ cup fresh or frozen peas
1 tablespoon minced fresh dill *or* 1 teaspoon dried dill weed
½ cup grated Parmesan cheese
1 teaspoon grated lemon peel

1. Combine broth and pepper in medium saucepan. Bring to a simmer over medium-high heat; keep warm over low heat.

2. Heat oil in large saucepan over medium-low heat. Add rice; cook and stir 1 minute. Stir ⅔ cup hot broth into saucepan; cook until broth is absorbed, stirring constantly.

3. Stir in remaining hot broth, ½ cup at a time, stirring frequently until broth is absorbed before adding next ½ cup. When last ½ cup broth is added, stir in spinach, peas and dill. Cook, stirring gently, until all broth is absorbed and rice is just tender but still firm. (Total cooking time will be about 20 minutes.)

4. Remove from heat; stir in Parmesan and lemon peel. *Makes 6 servings*

Note: Arborio rice, an Italian-grown short-grain rice, has large, plump grains with a delicious nutty taste. It is traditionally used for risotto dishes because its high starch content produces a creamy texture.

RISOTTO ALLA MILANESE

- **¼ teaspoon saffron threads**
- **3½ to 4 cups chicken or vegetable broth**
- **4 tablespoons butter, divided**
- **1 large onion, chopped**
- **1½ cups uncooked arborio or short-grain white rice**
- **½ cup dry white wine**
- **½ teaspoon salt**
- **Dash black pepper**
- **¼ cup grated Parmesan cheese**
- **Chopped fresh parsley**

1. Crush saffron to a powder; place in glass measuring cup.

2. Bring broth to a simmer in medium saucepan over medium heat; keep warm over low heat. Stir ½ cup broth into saffron to dissolve; set aside.

3. Heat 3 tablespoons butter in large saucepan over medium heat until melted and bubbly. Add onion; cook and stir 5 minutes or until onion is soft. Add rice; cook and stir 2 minutes. Stir in wine, salt and pepper; cook over medium-high heat 3 to 5 minutes until wine is absorbed, stirring occasionally.

4. Reduce heat to medium-low. Stir ½ cup hot broth into rice mixture; cook and stir until broth is absorbed. Repeat, adding ½ cup broth three more times, cooking and stirring until broth is absorbed.

5. Add saffron-flavored broth to rice; cook until absorbed. Continue to add remaining broth, ½ cup at a time, cooking and stirring until rice is tender but firm and mixture has slight creamy consistency. (Not all broth may be necessary. Total cooking time will be 20 to 25 minutes.)

6. Remove risotto from heat. Stir in remaining 1 tablespoon butter and Parmesan. Sprinkle with parsley. Serve immediately.

Makes 6 to 8 servings

WILD MUSHROOM RISOTTO

1 cup sliced portobello mushrooms
1 cup sliced shiitake mushrooms, stems discarded
½ cup finely chopped onion
2 tablespoons FRENCH'S® Worcestershire Sauce
2 cups uncooked arborio rice or white rice
2 cans (10½ ounces each) condensed chicken broth
½ cup frozen baby peas
½ cup (2 ounces) grated Parmesan cheese

1. Heat *1 tablespoon oil* in 5-quart saucepot or Dutch oven over medium-high heat. Add mushrooms and onion. Cook and stir 3 minutes or until mushrooms are tender. Add Worcestershire. Cook, stirring, until liquid is absorbed.

2. Add rice; cook 2 minutes, stirring constantly. Combine broth and *2½ cups water.* Add *4 cups* liquid to rice. Heat to boiling. Reduce heat to medium-low. Cook, uncovered, 8 minutes or until liquid is absorbed, stirring often. Add remaining broth, *½ cup* at a time. Cook and stir until rice is firm but tender and creamy.

3. Stir in peas and cheese; cook 1 minute. Serve with tossed green salad, if desired.

Makes 4 servings

Prep Time: 5 minutes **Cook Time:** about 15 minutes

Tip Arborio is one of the best varieties of rice for risotto. It is a translucent short-grain Italian rice; its high starch content helps produce the characteristic creamy texture of the dish.

WINTER SQUASH RISOTTO

4 to 5 cups vegetable broth
2 tablespoons olive oil
1 small butternut squash or 1 medium delicata squash, peeled and cut into 1-inch pieces (about 2 cups)
1 large shallot or small onion, finely chopped
½ teaspoon paprika
¼ teaspoon dried thyme
¼ teaspoon salt
¼ teaspoon black pepper
1 cup uncooked arborio rice
¼ cup dry white wine (optional)
½ cup grated Parmesan or Romano cheese

1. Bring broth to a simmer in medium saucepan over medium heat; keep warm over low heat.

2. Heat oil in large skillet over medium heat. Add squash; cook and stir 3 minutes. Add shallot; cook and stir 3 to 4 minutes or until squash is almost tender. Stir in paprika, thyme, salt and pepper. Add rice; stir to coat.

3. Add wine, if desired; cook and stir until wine is absorbed. Add ½ cup broth; cook until almost dry, stirring occasionally. Repeat with remaining broth. Rice is done when consistency is creamy and grains are tender with slight resistance. (Total cooking time will be 20 to 30 minutes.)

4. Sprinkle with Parmesan just before serving.

Makes 4 to 6 servings

ASPARAGUS–PARMESAN RISOTTO

5½ cups vegetable broth
⅛ teaspoon salt
4 tablespoons unsalted butter, divided
⅓ cup finely chopped onion
2 cups uncooked arborio rice
⅔ cup dry white wine
2½ cups fresh asparagus pieces (about 1 inch long)
⅔ cup frozen peas
1 cup grated Parmesan cheese

1. Bring broth and salt to a simmer in medium saucepan over medium heat; keep warm over low heat.

2. Melt 3 tablespoons butter in large saucepan over medium heat. Add onion; cook and stir 2 to 3 minutes or until tender. Stir in rice; cook 2 minutes or until rice is coated with butter, stirring frequently. Add wine; cook, stirring occasionally, until most of wine is absorbed.

3. Add 1½ cups hot broth; cook and stir 6 to 7 minutes or until most of liquid is absorbed. (Mixture should simmer but not boil.) Add 2 cups broth and asparagus; cook and stir 6 to 7 minutes or until most of liquid is absorbed. Add remaining 2 cups broth and peas; cook and stir 5 to 6 minutes or until most of liquid is absorbed and rice mixture is creamy.

4. Remove from heat; stir in remaining 1 tablespoon butter and Parmesan until melted.

Makes 4 to 5 servings

Asparagus-Spinach Risotto: Substitute 1 cup baby spinach leaves or chopped spinach for peas. Proceed as directed.

Asparagus-Chicken Risotto: Add 2 cups chopped or shredded cooked chicken to risotto with peas in step 3. Proceed as directed.

Tip: The broth can be added in smaller increments of ½ to ¾ cup, if desired. Just be sure to stir the rice mixture constantly for a creamy texture.

VEGETABLE RISOTTO

3 cups vegetable broth
2 tablespoons olive oil, divided
1 medium zucchini, cubed
1 medium yellow squash, cubed
1 cup chopped onion
1 cup sliced stemmed shiitake mushrooms
1 clove garlic, minced
3 plum tomatoes, seeded and chopped
1 teaspoon dried oregano
1 cup arborio rice
¼ cup grated Parmesan cheese
Salt and black pepper
½ cup frozen peas, thawed

1. Bring broth to a simmer in small saucepan over medium heat; keep warm over low heat.

2. Heat 1 tablespoon oil in large saucepan over medium heat. Add zucchini and yellow squash; cook and stir 5 minutes or until crisp-tender. Transfer to medium bowl; set aside.

3. Add onion, mushrooms and garlic to saucepan; cook and stir 5 minutes or until tender. Add tomatoes and oregano; cook and stir 2 to 3 minutes or until tomatoes are softened. Transfer to bowl with zucchini mixture.

4. Heat remaining 1 tablespoon oil in same saucepan over medium heat. Add rice; cook and stir 2 minutes.

5. Add ¾ cup broth to rice; cook and stir until broth is absorbed. Repeat with remaining broth. Cook until rice is tender but still firm. (Total cooking time will be 20 to 25 minutes.)

6. Stir in Parmesan; season with salt and pepper. Stir in reserved vegetables and peas; cook until heated through. Serve immediately.

Makes 4 to 6 servings

FIVE MUSHROOM RISOTTO

4 cups vegetable broth
4 tablespoons olive oil, divided
2 tablespoons butter
1 shallot, minced
¼ cup fresh Italian parsley, minced
¼ cup dry white wine
½ cup *each* shiitake, chanterelle, portobello, oyster and button mushrooms, wiped clean and chopped into ½-inch pieces
½ teaspoon coarse salt
1 cup arborio rice
½ cup whipping cream
¼ cup grated Parmesan cheese
Salt and black pepper
White truffle oil (optional)

1. Bring broth to a simmer in medium saucepan over medium heat; keep warm over low heat.

2. Heat 2 tablespoons oil and butter in large saucepan over medium-high heat. Add shallot; cook and stir 30 seconds or just until beginning to brown. Add parsley; cook and stir 30 seconds.

3. Add wine; cook and stir until wine evaporates. Add mushrooms and coarse salt; cook and stir until mushrooms have softened and reduced their volume by half. Transfer mushroom mixture to medium bowl; set aside.

4. Heat remaining 2 tablespoons oil in same saucepan. Add rice; cook and stir 1 to 2 minutes or until edges of rice become translucent.

5. Reduce heat to medium-low. Add ½ cup broth, stirring constantly until broth is absorbed. Repeat until only ½ cup broth remains. Stir mushroom mixture into rice. Add remaining broth; cook and stir until absorbed.

6. Remove from heat; add cream and Parmesan, stirring until Parmesan is melted. Season with salt and pepper. Drizzle with truffle oil, if desired.

Makes 4 servings

BAKED RISOTTO WITH ASPARAGUS, SPINACH & PARMESAN

1 tablespoon olive oil
1 cup finely chopped onion
1 cup uncooked arborio rice
8 cups (8 to 10 ounces) packed torn stemmed spinach
2 cups vegetable broth
¼ teaspoon salt
¼ teaspoon ground nutmeg
½ cup grated Parmesan cheese, divided
1½ cups diagonally sliced asparagus

1. Preheat oven to 400°F. Grease 13×9-inch baking dish.

2. Heat oil in large skillet over medium-high heat. Add onion; cook and stir 4 minutes or until tender. Add rice; stir to coat with oil.

3. Stir in spinach, a handful at a time, adding more as it wilts. Add broth, salt and nutmeg. Reduce heat and simmer 7 minutes. Stir in ¼ cup Parmesan. Transfer to prepared baking dish; cover tightly with foil.

4. Bake 15 minutes. Remove from oven; stir in asparagus and sprinkle with remaining ¼ cup cheese. Cover and bake 15 minutes or until liquid is absorbed.

Makes 6 servings

GARDEN-STYLE RISOTTO

1 can (14½ ounces) low-sodium chicken broth
1¾ cups water
2 cloves garlic, finely chopped
1 teaspoon dried basil leaves, crushed
½ teaspoon dried thyme leaves, crushed
1 cup arborio rice
2 cups packed DOLE® Baby Spinach
1 cup shredded DOLE® Carrots
3 tablespoons grated Parmesan cheese

• Combine broth, water, garlic, basil and thyme in large saucepan; bring to boil. Meanwhile, prepare rice.

• Place rice in large nonstick saucepan sprayed with vegetable cooking spray. Cook and stir rice over medium heat about 2 minutes or until rice is browned.

• Pour 1 cup boiling broth into saucepan with rice; cook, stirring constantly, until broth is almost absorbed (there should be some broth left).

• Add enough broth to barely cover rice; continue to cook, stirring constantly, until broth is almost absorbed. Repeat adding broth and cooking, stirring constantly, until broth is almost absorbed, about 15 minutes; add spinach and carrots with the last addition of broth.

• Cook 3 to 5 minutes more, stirring constantly, or until broth is almost absorbed and rice and vegetables are tender. Do not overcook. (Risotto will be saucy and have a creamy texture.) Stir in Parmesan cheese. Serve warm. *Makes 6 servings*

Garden Pilaf: Substitute 1 cup uncooked long grain white rice for arborio rice and reduce water from 1¾ cups to ½ cup. Prepare broth as directed above with ½ cup water; meanwhile, brown rice as directed above. Carefully add browned rice to boiling broth. Reduce heat to low; cover and cook 15 minutes. Stir in vegetables; cover and cook 4 to 5 minutes longer or until rice and vegetables are tender. Stir in Parmesan cheese.

Prep Time: 5 minutes **Cook Time:** 25 minutes

CREAMY RISOTTO PRIMAVERA

1½ cups sliced fresh mushrooms
½ cup chopped onion
½ cup diced carrots
2 cloves garlic, minced
2 tablespoons olive oil
1 cup arborio rice
3 cups water
1 tablespoon HERB-OX® chicken flavored bouillon
½ cup sherry or white cooking wine
1 cup shredded Fontina cheese
¼ cup grated Parmesan cheese
Chopped fresh parsley, for garnish
Diced fresh tomato

In large saucepan, sauté mushrooms, onion, carrot and garlic in hot oil until onion is tender. Add uncooked rice. Cook and stir over medium heat 3 to 5 minutes or until rice is golden brown. Meanwhile, in another saucepan, heat water, bouillon and wine to a boil. Slowly add 1 cup of broth to rice mixture, stirring constantly. Continue to cook and stir over medium heat until liquid is absorbed. Continue to add ½ cup of broth at a time to rice mixture, stirring constantly, until all broth has been added, absorbed and rice mixture is creamy. Add cheeses and stir until well blended. Garnish as desired with fresh parsley and diced tomato. *Makes 6 servings*

FAMILY FAVORITES

Table of Contents

Everyday Entrées

ROASTED SAUSAGE WITH WHITE BEANS

1 pound (4 links) Italian sausage
2 tablespoons extra virgin olive oil
10 fresh sage leaves (about 1 sprig)
2 cloves garlic, minced
1 can (about 14 ounces) diced tomatoes
2 cans (about 15 ounces each) cannellini beans, rinsed and drained
¼ teaspoon salt
⅛ teaspoon black pepper

1. Preheat oven to 400°F. Line rimmed baking sheet with foil. Arrange sausages on prepared baking sheet; roast about 18 minutes or until sausages are cooked through.

2. Heat oil in large skillet over medium-low heat. Add sage and garlic; cook 2 to 3 minutes or just until garlic begins to turn golden. Add tomatoes; bring to a simmer.

3. Stir in beans, salt and pepper; simmer 15 minutes. Serve sausages over beans.

Makes 4 servings

Note: The sausages can be grilled instead of roasted.

MINESTRONE SKILLET DINNER

2 slices bacon, coarsely chopped
1 tablespoon olive oil
2 cups coarsely shredded or chopped cabbage
1 large zucchini, cut into ½-inch pieces
1 medium onion, chopped
¾ cup chopped carrots
1 stalk celery, chopped
1 clove garlic, minced
1 can (about 14 ounces) diced tomatoes
1 cup cooked whole wheat macaroni
¾ cup canned Great Northern or cannellini beans, rinsed and drained
½ teaspoon dried oregano
¼ teaspoon salt
¼ teaspoon dried thyme
⅔ cup shredded Parmesan cheese

1. Preheat oven to 350°F. Cook bacon in large ovenproof skillet over medium heat until crisp. Remove bacon; drain on paper towels.

2. Add oil to skillet; heat over medium-high heat. Add cabbage, zucchini, onion, carrots, celery and garlic; cook and stir 10 minutes or until cabbage is crisp-tender.

3. Stir in tomatoes, macaroni, beans, oregano, salt, thyme and bacon; simmer 5 minutes. Sprinkle with Parmesan.

4. Bake 15 minutes or until hot and bubbly. *Makes 6 servings*

Tip: For a vegetarian dish, omit the bacon and increase the olive oil to 1½ tablespoons.

POLENTA WITH SAUTÉED MUSHROOMS

1 cup milk
1 cup chicken or vegetable broth
⅔ cup yellow cornmeal
½ teaspoon plus ⅛ teaspoon salt, divided
1 tablespoon olive oil
2 packages (4 ounces each) sliced mixed exotic mushrooms *or* 8 ounces cremini mushrooms, sliced
3 cloves garlic, minced
1 teaspoon dried thyme
¼ teaspoon black pepper
¼ cup red or port wine
½ cup grated Parmesan cheese, divided
Fresh thyme (optional)

1. Whisk milk, broth, cornmeal and ½ teaspoon salt in medium saucepan. Bring to a boil over high heat. Reduce heat to medium-low; simmer 10 minutes or until thickened, whisking occasionally.

2. Meanwhile, heat oil in large skillet over medium heat. Add mushrooms, garlic, thyme, pepper and remaining ⅛ teaspoon salt; cook and stir 6 minutes. Add wine; simmer 4 minutes or until liquid is reduced and mushrooms are tender.

3. Stir ¼ cup Parmesan into polenta. Transfer to serving plates; top with mushroom mixture and remaining ¼ cup Parmesan. Garnish with fresh thyme.

Makes 4 servings

MILANESE PORK CHOPS

2 tablespoons all-purpose flour
½ teaspoon salt
½ teaspoon black pepper
1 egg
1 teaspoon water
¼ cup seasoned dry bread crumbs
¼ cup grated Parmesan cheese
4 boneless pork loin chops, cut ¾ inch thick
1 tablespoon olive oil
1 tablespoon butter
Lemon wedges

1. Preheat oven to 400°F. Combine flour, salt and pepper in shallow dish. Beat egg and water in shallow bowl. Combine bread crumbs and Parmesan in separate shallow dish.

2. Dip each pork chop to coat both sides evenly, first in flour mixture, then egg mixture, then in bread crumb mixture. Press coating onto pork. Place on waxed paper; refrigerate 15 minutes or up to 1 hour.

3. Heat oil and butter in large ovenproof skillet over medium-high heat until bubbly. Add chops; cook 4 minutes or until golden brown. Turn chops and transfer skillet to oven. Bake 6 to 8 minutes or until cooked through (145°F). Serve with lemon wedges.

Makes 4 servings

CHICKEN PARMESAN STROMBOLI

1 pound boneless, skinless chicken breast halves
½ teaspoon salt
¼ teaspoon ground black pepper
2 teaspoons olive oil
2 cups shredded mozzarella cheese (about 8 ounces)
1 jar (1 pound 8 ounces) RAGÚ® Chunky Pasta Sauce, divided
2 tablespoons grated Parmesan cheese
1 tablespoon finely chopped fresh parsley
1 pound fresh or thawed frozen bread dough

1. Preheat oven to 400°F. Season chicken with salt and pepper. In 12-inch skillet, heat olive oil over medium-high heat and brown chicken. Remove chicken from skillet and let cool; pull into large shreds.

2. In medium bowl, combine chicken, mozzarella cheese, ½ cup Pasta Sauce, Parmesan cheese and parsley; set aside.

3. On greased jelly-roll pan, press dough to form 12×10-inch rectangle. Arrange chicken mixture down center of dough. Cover filling by bringing one long side of dough into center, then overlap with the other long side; pinch seam to seal. Fold in ends and pinch to seal. Arrange on pan, seam-side down. Gently press in sides to form 12×4-inch loaf. Bake 35 minutes or until dough is cooked and golden. Cut stromboli into slices. Heat remaining pasta sauce and serve with stromboli.

Makes 6 servings

GRILLED STEAK WITH ARUGULA & GORGONZOLA SALAD

4 boneless beef top loin (strip) steaks (¾ inch thick)
1 cup balsamic or red wine vinaigrette, divided
2 cups mixed salad greens
1½ cups baby arugula leaves
½ cup crumbled Gorgonzola cheese

1. Combine steaks and ½ cup vinaigrette in large resealable food storage bag. Seal bag; turn to coat. Marinate in refrigerator 20 to 30 minutes.

2. Preheat grill. Remove steaks from marinade; discard marinade. Grill, covered, over medium-high heat 6 to 8 minutes for medium-rare (145°F) or until desired doneness, turning once.

3. Meanwhile, combine salad greens and arugula in medium bowl. Pour remaining ½ cup vinaigrette over greens; toss until well coated. Serve steaks with salad. Sprinkle with Gorgonzola. *Makes 4 servings*

ITALIAN SAUSAGE & VEGETABLE STEW

1 pound hot or mild Italian sausage links, cut into 1-inch pieces
1 package (16 ounces) frozen vegetable blend, such as onions and green, red and yellow bell peppers
2 medium zucchini, sliced
1 can (about 14 ounces) Italian-style diced tomatoes
1 jar (4½ ounces) sliced mushrooms, drained
4 cloves garlic, minced

1. Brown sausage in large saucepan over medium-high heat 5 minutes, stirring frequently; drain fat.

2. Add frozen vegetables, zucchini, tomatoes, mushrooms and garlic; bring to a boil. Reduce heat to medium-low; cover and simmer 10 minutes. Uncover; cook 5 to 10 minutes or until slightly thickened. *Makes 6 servings*

STEAK WITH ARUGULA & GORGONZOLA SALAD

PORK SCALOPPINE

- **⅓ cup all-purpose flour**
- **¾ teaspoon salt**
- **½ teaspoon black pepper**
- **1 pound pork tenderloin, cut into ½-inch-thick slices**
- **3 tablespoons olive oil, divided**
- **16 ounces sliced mushrooms**
- **½ cup sliced green onions**
- **½ cup water**
- **¼ cup white wine**
- **½ teaspoon dried marjoram**
- **½ teaspoon dried basil**
- **½ cup chopped pimiento-stuffed green olives**
- **8 ounces orzo pasta, cooked**

1. Combine flour, salt and pepper in shallow bowl. Pound pork slices to ¼-inch thickness with meat mallet. Dip each slice in flour to coat both sides; shake off excess flour.

2. Heat 1 tablespoon oil in large skillet over medium-high heat. Add mushrooms; cook and stir 6 to 8 minutes or until tender. Remove from skillet and keep warm.

3. Heat remaining 2 tablespoons oil in same skillet. Add pork; cook 1 to 2 minutes per side or until browned. Add green onions, water, wine, marjoram and basil; bring to a simmer. Stir in olives; cover and cook 3 to 4 minutes per side or until pork is no longer pink in center. Remove pork to serving platter.

4. Return mushrooms along with any accumulated juices to skillet; cook 2 to 3 minutes or until heated through. Pour sauce over pork; serve with hot cooked orzo.

Makes 4 to 6 servings

CHICKEN WITH PARMESAN FETTUCCINE

2 tablespoons butter, divided
1 pound boneless skinless chicken breasts, cut into bite-size pieces
1 clove garlic, minced
3½ cups chicken broth or water
6 ounces uncooked fettuccine, broken in half
½ cup whipping cream
½ cup grated Parmesan cheese
½ cup finely chopped green onions
¼ teaspoon black pepper

1. Melt 1 tablespoon butter in large saucepan over medium heat. Add chicken and garlic; cook and stir 3 minutes or until cooked through. Remove chicken and keep warm.

2. Add broth to saucepan; bring to boil over high heat. Add pasta; return to a boil. Reduce heat to medium-low; cover and simmer 10 minutes or just until tender. Drain pasta and return to saucepan, reserving 2 tablespoons broth.

3. Add chicken along with any accumulated juices and cream to pasta. Gradually stir in Parmesan cheese. Stir in green onions, pepper and remaining 1 tablespoon butter; cook and stir 2 minutes or until thickened. Add reserved broth to thin sauce, if necessary. *Makes 4 servings*

Tip: Just before serving, toss in steamed asparagus or any steamed vegetable; stir to coat.

PORK CHOPS WITH VINEGAR PEPPERS

4 pork rib chops (about 1 inch thick)
½ teaspoon salt
¼ teaspoon black pepper
2 tablespoons olive oil
1½ cups seeded hot cherry peppers cut into ½-inch slices*
2 cloves garlic, minced
¼ cup liquid from cherry pepper jar
¼ cup water
1 sprig fresh rosemary
Chopped fresh Italian parsley (optional)

**Hot cherry peppers are also available presliced in rings.*

1. Pat pork chops dry with paper towels. Season both sides with salt and pepper.

2. Heat oil in large saucepan over medium-high heat. Add pork chops; cook about 5 minutes per side or until browned. Remove from skillet; keep warm.

3. Add cherry peppers and garlic to skillet; cook and stir 2 minutes over medium heat, scraping up browned bits from bottom of pan. Stir in cherry pepper liquid, water and rosemary.

4. Return pork chops along with any accumulated juices to skillet; cover and cook about 6 minutes or until pork is barely pink in center. Sprinkle with parsley, if desired.

Makes 4 servings

CHICKEN CACCIATORE

8 ounces uncooked rigatoni or penne pasta
1 can (about 15 ounces) chunky Italian-style tomato sauce
1 cup sliced onion
1 cup sliced mushrooms
1 cup chopped green bell pepper
1 tablespoon olive oil
4 boneless skinless chicken breasts (about 1 pound)
Salt and black pepper

1. Cook pasta according to package directions; drain and keep warm.

2. Meanwhile, combine tomato sauce, onion, mushrooms and bell pepper in large microwavable dish. Cover loosely with plastic wrap or waxed paper; microwave on HIGH 6 to 8 minutes, stirring halfway through cooking time.

3. Heat oil in large skillet over medium-high heat. Cook chicken 3 to 4 minutes per side or until lightly browned.

4. Add tomato sauce mixture to skillet; season with salt and pepper. Reduce heat to medium; simmer 12 to 15 minutes. Serve over pasta.

Makes 4 servings

Tip

Pasta should be cooked in plenty of rapidly boiling water—for 1 pound of pasta, use 4 to 6 quarts of water and 2 teaspoons of salt. Stir the pasta gently after adding it until the water returns to a boil; this will keep it from sticking. Always check the package for the manufacturer's recommended cooking time and begin testing for doneness at the minimum recommended time When the pasta is tender but still firm (al dente), it's done.

Vegetables & Sides

PROSCIUTTO PROVOLONE ROLLS

1 loaf (16 ounces) frozen bread dough, thawed
¼ cup garlic and herb spreadable cheese
6 thin slices prosciutto (3-ounce package)
6 slices (1 ounce each) provolone cheese

1. Spray 12 standard (2½-inch) muffin cups with nonstick cooking spray. Roll out dough on lightly floured surface into 12×10-inch rectangle.

2. Spread garlic and herb cheese evenly over dough. Arrange prosciutto slices over herb cheese; top with provolone slices. Starting with long side, roll up dough jelly-roll style; pinch seam to seal.

3. Cut crosswise into 1-inch slices; arrange slices, cut side down, in prepared muffin cups. Cover; let rise in warm place 30 to 40 minutes or until nearly doubled.

4. Preheat oven to 350°F. Bake rolls about 18 minutes or until golden brown. Loosen edges of rolls with knife; remove from pan to wire rack. Serve warm.

Makes 12 rolls

GARLIC & HERB POLENTA

3 tablespoons butter, divided
8 cups water
2 cups yellow cornmeal
2 teaspoons salt
2 teaspoons finely minced garlic
3 tablespoons chopped fresh herbs such as parsley, chives or thyme (or a combination)

Slow Cooker Directions

Grease inside of slow cooker with 1 tablespoon butter. Add water, cornmeal, salt, garlic and remaining 2 tablespoons butter; stir. Cover; cook on LOW 4 hours or on HIGH 3 hours, stirring occasionally. Stir in herbs just before serving.

Makes 6 servings

Tip: Polenta may also be poured into a greased pan and allowed to cool until set. Cut into squares or slices to serve, or chill polenta slices until firm and then grill or fry until golden brown.

PEAS FLORENTINE STYLE

2 (10-ounce) packages frozen peas
¼ cup FILIPPO BERIO® Olive Oil
4 ounces Canadian bacon, cubed
1 garlic clove, minced
1 tablespoon chopped fresh Italian parsley
1 teaspoon sugar
Salt

Place peas in large colander or strainer; run under hot water until slightly thawed. Drain well. In medium skillet, heat olive oil over medium heat until hot. Add bacon and garlic; cook and stir 2 to 3 minutes or until garlic turns golden. Add peas and parsley; cook and stir over high heat 5 to 7 minutes or until heated through. Drain well. Stir in sugar; season to taste with salt.

Makes 5 servings

ROASTED PEPPERS & POTATOES

2 pounds small red potatoes, quartered
1 large red bell pepper, cut into 1½-inch chunks
1 large yellow or orange bell pepper, cut into 1½-inch chunks
1 large red onion, cut into 1-inch pieces
¼ cup olive oil
3 cloves garlic, minced
¾ teaspoon salt
¼ teaspoon black pepper
¼ teaspoon dried basil
¼ teaspoon dried oregano

1. Preheat oven to 375°F.

2. Place potatoes, bell peppers and onion in large bowl. Combine oil, garlic, salt, black pepper, basil and oregano in small bowl; pour over vegetables. Stir until vegetables are evenly coated. Spread on large baking sheet.

3. Bake 50 minutes or until potatoes are tender and beginning to brown, stirring every 15 minutes. *Makes 4 to 6 servings*

OVEN ROASTED TOMATOES

6 ripe plum or vine tomatoes
1 teaspoon freeze-dried oregano
2 cloves garlic, crushed
Salt and freshly ground black pepper
5 tablespoons FILIPPO BERIO® Olive Oil

Preheat the oven to 375°F. Cut the tomatoes in half and place cut side up in a single layer in a large ovenproof dish. Scatter the oregano, garlic and plenty of salt and pepper over the tomatoes. Drizzle with the olive oil. Bake for 30 to 35 minutes or until the tomatoes have softened. *Makes 4 servings*

COUNTRY POLENTA

4 cups water
½ teaspoon salt (optional)
2 cups CREAM OF WHEAT® Hot Cereal (Instant, 1-minute, 2½-minute or 10-minute cook time), uncooked, divided
⅓ cup grated Parmesan cheese
¼ teaspoon crushed red pepper
¼ teaspoon dried basil
¼ teaspoon ground black pepper
3 tablespoons vegetable oil

1. Coat 8-inch square pan generously with nonstick cooking spray. Bring water and salt, if desired, to a boil. Gradually add 1 cup Cream of Wheat, stirring constantly with wire whisk until well blended. Return to a boil. Reduce heat to low; simmer, uncovered, as directed on package or until thickened, stirring frequently. Cool slightly.

2. Add cheese, red pepper, basil and black pepper; mix well. Pour Cream of Wheat mixture evenly into prepared pan; cover. Refrigerate at least 2 hours or until set.

3. Toast remaining 1 cup Cream of Wheat in large skillet over medium-low heat until golden brown, stirring frequently. Remove from heat. Cut chilled polenta into 12 triangles. Coat both sides generously with toasted Cream of Wheat.

4. Heat oil in large skillet over medium heat. Cook polenta triangles 3 to 4 minutes on each side or until crisp and golden brown. Serve immediately.

Makes 6 servings

Tip: Prepared Cream of Wheat mixture can be poured into pan, tightly covered and refrigerated up to 24 hours before being cut into triangles. Coat with toasted cereal; proceed as directed.

Prep Time: 15 minutes ✦ **Start to Finish Time:** 2 hours 25 minutes

QUICK ZUCCHINI PARMESAN

2 teaspoons olive oil
2 large zucchini or yellow squash, cut into ¼-inch thick slices (4 cups)
2 cloves garlic, minced
¼ teaspoon salt
¼ teaspoon black pepper
¼ cup grated Parmesan cheese
¼ cup thinly sliced basil

1. Heat oil in large nonstick skillet over medium heat. Add zucchini; cook and stir 2 minutes.

2. Add garlic, salt and pepper; cook 4 to 5 minutes or just until zucchini is tender. Top with Parmesan and basil. *Makes 4 servings*

BROCCOLI ITALIAN STYLE

1¼ pounds fresh broccoli
2 tablespoons lemon juice
1 tablespoon extra virgin olive oil
1 clove garlic, minced
1 teaspoon chopped fresh Italian parsley
Dash black pepper

1. Trim broccoli, discarding tough stems. Cut broccoli into florets with 2-inch stems. Peel remaining stems; cut into ½-inch slices.

2. Bring 1 quart water to a boil in large saucepan over medium-high heat. Add broccoli; return to a boil. Cook 3 to 5 minutes or until broccoli is tender. Drain and transfer to serving dish.

3. Combine lemon juice, oil, garlic, parsley and pepper in small bowl. Pour over broccoli; toss to coat. Cover and let stand 1 hour before serving to allow flavors to blend. Serve at room temperature. *Makes 4 servings*

Pasta Perfection

FARFALLE WITH GARLIC VEGETABLES

3 medium carrots, thinly sliced
2 small zucchini, thinly sliced
¼ cup (½ stick) butter
1 large onion, chopped
4 cloves garlic, minced
½ cup vegetable broth
½ cup whipping cream
½ teaspoon salt
½ teaspoon dried basil
¼ teaspoon black pepper
2 cups hot cooked farfalle pasta

1. Place carrots and zucchini in large saucepan; add water to cover. Cook, uncovered, 3 minutes or until crisp-tender. Drain and set aside.

2. Melt butter in same saucepan. Add onion and garlic; cook and stir until tender. Gradually stir in broth, cream, salt, basil and pepper; simmer 5 minutes or until sauce is slightly thickened.

3. Add vegetables to saucepan; cook until heated through, stirring occasionally. Add pasta to sauce; toss lightly. Serve immediately.

Makes 4 servings

HANDKERCHIEF PASTA WITH CHICKEN & CHARD

2 bunches chard
8 ounces uncooked flat lasagna noodles
4 tablespoons plus 1 teaspoon extra virgin olive oil, divided
3 cloves garlic, minced
2 boneless skinless chicken breasts, cut into bite-size pieces
¼ cup balsamic vinegar
Salt and black pepper
Toasted pine nuts

1. Trim chard; pull leaves from large stems. Chop stems; roll leaves into bundles and slice into ribbons. Measure 9 loosely-packed cups; set aside.

2. Bring large saucepan of salted water to a boil. Break lasagna noodles into halves or thirds to make squares. (Don't worry if some pieces break unevenly.) Cook pasta in boiling water until tender but firm. Drain; toss lightly with 1 teaspoon oil to prevent sticking. Keep warm.

3. Heat 2 tablespoons oil in large skillet over medium heat. Add garlic; cook and stir 30 seconds. Add chicken; cook and stir about 2 minutes. Add remaining 2 tablespoons oil; stir in chard. Cover and cook until chard is wilted, stirring occasionally. Stir in vinegar; cook 3 to 5 minutes or until chicken is cooked through. Season with salt and pepper.

4. Divide pasta evenly among four serving plates; top with chicken mixture. Sprinkle with pine nuts.

Makes 4 servings

GARLIC SPINACH LASAGNA

12 uncooked lasagna noodles
2 tablespoons olive oil
4 cloves garlic, chopped
2 cups frozen chopped spinach, thawed and squeezed dry
Salt and black pepper
3 cups ricotta cheese
¾ cup plus 2 tablespoons grated Parmesan cheese, divided
2 eggs, lightly beaten
1 jar (about 24 ounces) pasta sauce
2 cups (8 ounces) shredded provolone or mozzarella cheese

1. Cook lasagna noodles according to package directions; drain and keep warm. Preheat oven to 350°F.

2. Heat oil in medium skillet over medium heat. Add garlic; cook 30 seconds. Add spinach, salt and pepper; cook and stir 3 minutes.

3. Combine ricotta, ¾ cup Parmesan and eggs in medium bowl; mix well.

4. Spread ¼ cup pasta sauce in bottom of 13×9-inch baking dish. Layer with four noodles, 1 cup sauce, half of ricotta mixture, half of spinach mixture and ½ cup provolone. Repeat layers. Top with remaining noodles, sauce, 1 cup provolone and 2 tablespoons Parmesan. Cover tightly with foil.

5. Bake 30 minutes or until hot and bubbly. Uncover and bake 15 minutes or until browned. Let stand 10 minutes before cutting. *Makes 8 servings*

ANGEL HAIR PASTA WITH SEAFOOD SAUCE

8 ounces uncooked angel hair pasta
2 teaspoons olive oil
½ cup chopped onion
2 cloves garlic, minced
3 pounds plum tomatoes, seeded and chopped
¼ cup chopped fresh basil
2 tablespoons chopped fresh oregano
1 teaspoon red pepper flakes
½ teaspoon sugar
2 bay leaves
½ pound firm whitefish, such as sea bass, monkfish or grouper, cut into ¾-inch pieces
½ pound bay scallops or shucked oysters
2 tablespoons chopped fresh Italian parsley

1. Cook pasta according to package directions; drain.

2. Heat oil in large nonstick skillet over medium heat. Add onion and garlic; cook and stir 3 minutes or until onion is translucent. Reduce heat to low. Add tomatoes, basil, oregano, red pepper flakes, sugar and bay leaves; cook 15 minutes, stirring occasionally.

3. Add whitefish and scallops; cook 3 to 4 minutes or until fish begins to flake when tested with fork and scallops are opaque. Remove and discard bay leaves.

4. Combine pasta and seafood sauce in large bowl; toss gently to coat. Sprinkle with parsley.

Makes 6 servings

PENNE WITH RICOTTA, TOMATOES & BASIL

16 ounces uncooked penne pasta
2 cans (about 14 ounces each) diced pasta-ready or Italian-seasoned tomatoes, drained
1 container (15 ounces) ricotta cheese
⅔ cup chopped fresh basil
¼ cup olive oil
1 tablespoon balsamic vinegar
1 clove garlic, minced
1 teaspoon salt
¼ teaspoon red pepper flakes or black pepper
Grated Parmesan cheese

1. Cook pasta according to package directions; drain.

2. Combine tomatoes, ricotta, basil, oil, vinegar, garlic, salt and red pepper flakes in large bowl; mix well.

3. Add pasta to ricotta mixture; toss gently to coat. Sprinkle with Parmesan. Serve immediately.

Makes 4 servings

Tip

Store garlic in a cool, dry, well-ventilated place away from light. Over time, garlic will develop small green shoots in the center of the cloves. These are not harmful but they may taste bitter, so it's best to remove them before using the garlic.

FUSILLI PIZZAIOLO

16 ounces uncooked rotini or fusilli pasta
¼ cup olive oil
8 ounces mushrooms, sliced
1 large red bell pepper, chopped
1 large green bell pepper, chopped
1 large yellow bell pepper, chopped
10 green onions, chopped
1 large onion, chopped
8 cloves garlic, minced
½ cup chopped fresh basil *or* 2 teaspoons dried basil
2 tablespoons chopped fresh oregano *or* 1 teaspoon dried oregano
Dash red pepper flakes
4 cups canned or fresh tomatoes, undrained and chopped
Salt and black pepper

1. Cook pasta according to package directions; drain and keep warm.

2. Heat oil in large skillet over medium-high heat. Add mushrooms, bell peppers, onions, garlic, basil, oregano and red pepper flakes; cook and stir until onion is lightly browned.

3. Add tomatoes with juice; bring to a boil. Reduce heat to low; simmer, uncovered, 20 minutes. Season with salt and black pepper.

4. Add pasta to sauce; toss to coat. *Makes 6 to 8 servings*

SPAGHETTI WITH ROASTED PEPPER & TOMATO SAUCE

1½ tablespoons olive oil
1 medium red onion, finely chopped
1 clove garlic, minced
Roasted Peppers* (recipe follows), chopped
1 can (about 14 ounces) fire-roasted diced tomatoes
½ teaspoon salt
¼ teaspoon dried oregano
¼ teaspoon red pepper flakes
⅛ teaspoon black pepper
8 ounces whole wheat spaghetti, cooked and drained
½ cup grated Parmesan cheese

**Or substitute 3 jarred roasted red bell peppers.*

1. Heat oil in large skillet over medium-high heat. Add onion and garlic; cook and stir 3 to 5 minutes or until tender. Add Roasted Peppers; cook 2 minutes.

2. Stir in tomatoes, salt, oregano, red pepper flakes and black pepper. Reduce heat to low; simmer 10 minutes. Serve over spaghetti; sprinkle with Parmesan.

Makes 4 servings

Roasted Peppers: Broil 3 large red bell peppers 4 inches from heat, turning frequently with long-handled tongs to blacken all sides. Transfer peppers to a large bowl and cover tightly, or place peppers in a paper bag and close the bag. Set aside for 30 minutes to 1 hour to loosen the skins. Scrape off the blackened skin with a paring knife.

SPICY ITALIAN SAUSAGE & PENNE PASTA

8 ounces uncooked penne pasta
1 pound bulk hot Italian sausage
1 cup chopped sweet onion
2 cloves garlic, minced
2 cans (about 14 ounces each) seasoned diced tomatoes
3 cups broccoli florets
½ cup shredded Asiago or Romano cheese

1. Cook pasta according to package directions; drain and keep warm in saucepan.

2. Crumble sausage into large skillet. Add onion; cook and stir over medium-high heat until sausage is cooked through. Drain fat. Add garlic; cook and stir 1 minute. Stir in tomatoes and broccoli; cover and cook 10 minutes or until broccoli is tender.

3. Add sausage mixture to pasta; toss to coat. Sprinkle with Asiago.

Makes 4 to 6 servings

Tip

Asiago is a rich, nutty-flavored Italian cheese made from cow's milk. It can have different textures depending on its age. Fresh Asiago is smooth and mild; it can be sliced for sandwiches or melted on casseroles. Mature Asiago (aged over one year) is more widely used; it has a yellower color and crumbly texture and is often grated into salads, pastas and sauces.

PASTA WITH CLASSIC BOLOGNESE SAUCE

- 2 tablespoons olive oil
- 1 medium onion, finely chopped
- 1 medium carrot, finely chopped
- 1 stalk celery, finely chopped
- 2 cloves garlic, minced
- 1 pound ground beef
- ¾ teaspoon salt, divided
- ½ teaspoon black pepper, divided
- 1 cup dry white wine, such as sauvignon blanc or pinot grigio
- 1 cup milk
- ⅛ teaspoon ground nutmeg
- 1 can (about 14 ounces) whole tomatoes, chopped, juice reserved
- 16 ounces uncooked pappardelle, tagliatelle or bucatini pasta
- 1 cup grated Parmesan cheese

1. Heat oil in medium saucepan over medium-high heat. Add onion; cook and stir 5 minutes or until translucent. Add carrot, celery and garlic; cook 5 to 7 minutes or until softened.

2. Add ground beef, ¼ teaspoon salt and ¼ teaspoon pepper; cook 7 minutes or until no longer pink, stirring to break up meat. Stir in wine; cook 10 minutes. Add milk and nutmeg; cook 10 minutes or until most of liquid has evaporated, stirring occasionally.

3. Add tomatoes and reserved juice; bring to a boil. Reduce heat to low; simmer, uncovered, 2 hours. Stir in remaining ½ teaspoon salt and ¼ teaspoon pepper.

4. Cook pasta according to package directions; drain. Combine pasta and sauce in large bowl; toss to coat. Sprinkle with Parmesan.

Makes 4 to 6 servings

Pizza & Panini

RUSTIC VEGETABLE PIZZA

1 (10-ounce) prepared whole wheat pizza crust
2 large plum tomatoes, thinly sliced
1 tablespoon olive oil
2 small zucchini, thinly sliced
1 small eggplant, peeled and thinly sliced
⅓ cup sliced red onion
¼ teaspoon garlic salt
¾ cup (3 ounces) shredded mozzarella cheese
1 tablespoon grated Romano cheese
3 tablespoons chopped fresh basil

1. Preheat oven to 450°F. Place pizza crust on baking sheet. Arrange tomatoes over crust.

2. Heat oil in large skillet over medium-high heat. Add zucchini, eggplant, onion and garlic salt; cook and stir 4 to 5 minutes or until crisp-tender. Layer vegetables over tomatoes on crust; top with mozzarella and Romano.

3. Bake 10 to 12 minutes or until cheeses are melted and crust is golden brown. Sprinkle with basil.

Makes 6 servings

GRILLED ITALIAN CHICKEN PANINI

6 small portobello mushroom caps (about 6 ounces)
½ cup plus 2 tablespoons balsamic vinaigrette dressing
1 loaf (16 ounces) Italian bread, cut into 12 slices
12 slices provolone cheese
1½ cups chopped cooked chicken
1 jar (12 ounces) roasted red peppers, drained

1. Brush mushrooms with 2 tablespoons dressing. Cook mushrooms in large nonstick skillet over medium-high heat 5 to 7 minutes or until soft. Cut diagonally into ½-inch slices.

2. For each sandwich, top one bread slice with one cheese slice, ¼ cup chicken, mushrooms, roasted red peppers, another cheese slice and another bread slice. Brush outsides of sandwiches with remaining dressing.

3. Preheat grill pan or panini press* over medium heat 5 minutes. Grill sandwiches 4 to 6 minutes or until cheese is melted and bread is golden, turning once.

Makes 6 sandwiches

**If you don't have a grill pan or panini press, grill sandwiches in a nonstick skillet. Place a clean heavy pan on top of sandwiches to weigh them down while cooking.*

Tip: A rotisserie chicken will yield just enough chopped chicken for this recipe.

HOMEMADE PIZZA MARGHERITA

Crust

2 cups all-purpose flour
1 cup whole wheat flour
2 teaspoons salt
1 package (¼ ounce) rapid-rise active dry yeast
1 cup hot water (120°F)
2 tablespoons extra virgin olive oil

Sauce*

1 tablespoon olive oil
1 onion, chopped
2 cloves garlic, minced
1 can (about 14 ounces) fire-roasted diced tomatoes
⅓ cup red wine (optional)
½ teaspoon Italian seasoning

Toppings

5 to 6 plum tomatoes, sliced
16 ounces fresh mozzarella cheese, thinly sliced
Fresh basil, torn into pieces

**Substitute prepared pizza sauce, if desired.*

1. Combine all-purpose flour, whole wheat flour, salt and yeast in food processor. Process with on/off pulses just until combined. With motor running, add water and 2 tablespoons oil through feed tube. Process 30 seconds or until dough forms a ball. Dough should be slightly sticky. If ball does not form and dough seems too wet, add additional all-purpose flour, 1 tablespoon at a time. If too dry, add water, 1 tablespoon at a time.

2. Place dough on floured surface; knead 1 minute. Transfer dough to oiled bowl; turn over to grease top. Cover; let rise in warm place 45 minutes or until almost doubled.**

3. For sauce, heat 1 tablespoon oil in medium saucepan over medium heat. Add onion and garlic; cook and stir 2 minutes or until softened. Add diced tomatoes, wine, if desired, and Italian seasoning; cook 5 to 10 minutes over

continued on page 248

Homemade Pizza Margherita, continued

medium-high heat or until slightly reduced, stirring occasionally. Remove from heat; let cool. Transfer to food processor; process with on/off pulses until almost smooth. Refrigerate until ready to use.

4. Preheat oven to 450°F. Punch down dough; place on floured surface. Divide into 2 or 3 pieces. Roll out each piece into 10- or 12-inch circle with floured rolling pin.

5. Transfer dough circles to baking sheets or pizza pans.*** Spread with thin layer of sauce. (Freeze leftover sauce for another use.) Top with plum tomatoes, mozzarella and basil.

6. Bake 6 to 10 minutes or until crust begins to brown around edges and toppings are bubbly. Transfer to cutting board. Top with additional basil before serving. *Makes 2 medium or 3 small pizzas*

***Dough may also be refrigerated for up to 24 hours for a slower rise. Bring dough to room temperature and proceed with recipe. Or wrap and freeze for up to 3 months.*

****Sprinkle baking sheets with cornmeal before transferring dough to prevent sticking.*

SICILIAN–STYLE PIZZA

2 loaves (1 pound each) frozen white bread dough
Vegetable cooking spray
1¾ cups PREGO® Traditional Italian Sauce
2 cups shredded mozzarella cheese (about 8 ounces)

1. Thaw the bread dough according to the package directions. Heat the oven to 375°F. Spray a 15×10-inch jelly-roll pan with cooking spray. Place the dough loaves into the pan. Press the dough from the center out until it covers the bottom of the pan. Pinch the edges of the dough to form a rim.

2. Spread the sauce over the crust. Top with the cheese.

3. Bake for 25 minutes or until the cheese is melted and the crust is golden.

Makes 8 servings

Tip: To thaw the dough more quickly, place the dough into a microwavable dish. Brush with melted butter or spray with vegetable cooking spray. Microwave on LOW for 1 to 2 minutes.

PORTOBELLO PANINI

6 to 8 ounces sliced portobello mushrooms
⅓ cup plus 1 tablespoon olive oil, divided
3 tablespoons balsamic vinegar
1 clove garlic, minced
½ teaspoon salt
¼ teaspoon black pepper
4 ciabatta rolls, split *or* 1 loaf (16 ounces) ciabatta or Italian bread
8 ounces sliced provolone cheese
¼ cup chopped fresh basil
8 ounces plum tomatoes, thinly sliced
3 tablespoons whole grain Dijon mustard

1. Place mushrooms, ⅓ cup oil, vinegar, garlic, salt and pepper in large resealable food storage bag. Seal tightly; shake to coat mushrooms evenly. Let stand 15 minutes, turning frequently. (Mushrooms may be prepared up to 24 hours in advance; refrigerate and turn occasionally.)

2. Preheat indoor grill. Brush outsides of rolls with remaining 1 tablespoon oil.

3. Arrange mushrooms evenly over bottom halves of rolls; drizzle with some of marinade. Top with provolone, basil and tomatoes. Spread mustard evenly over cut side of top halves of rolls; place over tomatoes.

4. Grill sandwiches 8 minutes or until bread is golden and cheese is melted. Wrap each sandwich tightly in foil to keep warm or serve at room temperature.

Makes 4 servings

CHICKEN–PESTO PIZZA

1 tablespoon olive oil
½ pound chicken tenders, cut into bite-size pieces
1 medium onion, thinly sliced
⅓ cup pesto sauce
3 medium plum tomatoes, thinly sliced
1 (14-inch) prepared pizza crust
1 cup (4 ounces) shredded mozzarella cheese

1. Preheat oven to 450°F. Heat oil in medium skillet over medium heat. Add chicken; cook and stir 2 minutes. Add onion and pesto; cook and stir about 3 minutes or until chicken is cooked through.

2. Arrange tomato slices and chicken mixture on pizza crust to within 1 inch of edge. Sprinkle with mozzarella.

3. Bake 8 minutes or until pizza is hot and cheese is melted and bubbly.

Makes 6 servings

SALAMI & PROVOLONE PANINI

8 slices Italian or white bread
12 slices Genoa or hard salami
8 slices provolone cheese
1 cup arugula or baby spinach leaves
¼ cup HELLMANN'S® or BEST FOODS® Mayonnaise Dressing with Extra Virgin Olive Oil

1. Evenly top 4 bread slices with salami, cheese and arugula, then remaining bread slices.

2. Brush both sides of sandwiches with HELLMANN'S® or BEST FOODS® Mayonnaise Dressing with Extra Virgin Olive Oil. In 12-inch skillet or grill pan, cook sandwiches over medium heat, turning once, 6 minutes or until bread is toasted and cheese is melted.

Makes 4 servings

Prep Time: 10 minutes ✦ **Cook Time:** 6 minutes

SAUSAGE, PEPPER & ONION PIZZA

½ cup tomato sauce
1 clove garlic, minced
½ teaspoon dried basil
½ teaspoon dried oregano
⅛ teaspoon red pepper flakes (optional)
2 grilled sausage links
1 grilled red onion
1 grilled or roasted bell pepper
1 (12-inch) prepared pizza crust
1½ cups (6 ounces) shredded fontina cheese or pizza cheese blend
½ cup grated Parmesan cheese

1. Preheat oven to 450°F. Combine tomato sauce, garlic, basil, oregano and red pepper flakes, if desired, in small bowl. Cut sausages in half lengthwise, then cut crosswise into ½-inch slices. Cut onion and bell pepper into 1-inch pieces.

2. Place pizza crust on pizza pan or baking sheet. Spread tomato sauce mixture over crust to within 1 inch of edge. Sprinkle fontina over tomato sauce; top with sausage, onion and bell pepper. Sprinkle with Parmesan.

3. Bake 12 minutes or until crust is crisp and cheeses are melted.

Makes 4 servings

PANINI WITH FRESH MOZZARELLA & BASIL

½ cup prepared vinaigrette
1 loaf (16 ounces) Italian bread, cut in half lengthwise
6 ounces fresh mozzarella cheese, cut into 12 slices
8 ounces thinly sliced oven-roasted deli turkey
12 to 16 fresh whole basil leaves
1 large tomato, thinly sliced
½ cup thinly sliced red onion
⅛ teaspoon red pepper flakes

1. Preheat indoor grill. Brush vinaigrette evenly over both cut sides of bread.

2. Arrange mozzarella evenly over bottom half of bread; top with turkey, basil, tomato and onion. Sprinkle with red pepper flakes. Cover with top half of bread; press down firmly. Cut into four sandwiches.

3. Grill sandwiches 5 to 7 minutes or until cheese is melted.

Makes 4 servings

ARTICHOKE PIZZA

2 teaspoons olive oil
1 cup thinly sliced mushrooms
½ cup thinly sliced onion
1 (6-inch) prepared pizza crust
½ cup thinly sliced artichoke hearts (not marinated in oil), drained
½ cup (2 ounces) shredded Italian blend cheese

1. Preheat oven to 450°F. Heat oil in medium skillet over medium heat. Add mushrooms and onion; cook and stir about 10 minutes until vegetables are tender but not browned. Spread on pizza crust.

2. Top pizza with artichoke hearts and cheese. Bake 8 to 10 minutes or until cheese is melted.

Makes 1 to 2 servings

CLASSIC POTATO, ONION & HAM PIZZA

3 tablespoons butter or olive oil, divided
3 cups new potatoes, cut into ¼-inch slices
2 sweet onions, cut into ¼-inch slices
1 tablespoon coarsely chopped garlic
½ teaspoon salt
½ teaspoon black pepper
2 cups (8 ounces) shredded Wisconsin Mozzarella cheese
1 (16-ounce) Italian-style bread shell pizza crust
8 thin slices (4 ounces) deli ham
8 slices (4 ounces) Wisconsin Provolone cheese
⅓ cup grated Wisconsin Parmesan cheese
¼ cup chopped Italian parsley

Melt 2 tablespoons butter or olive oil in large skillet over medium heat; add potatoes, onions, garlic, salt and pepper. Cook 12 to 15 minutes, turning occasionally. Add remaining 1 tablespoon butter. Cook 5 to 7 minutes or until potatoes are golden brown. Cool slightly.

Preheat oven to 400°F. Sprinkle mozzarella cheese over crust; top with ham slices. Arrange potato mixture over ham; top with provolone cheese. Sprinkle with Parmesan cheese and parsley. Place crust directly on oven rack; bake for 15 to 20 minutes or until cheese is melted. *Makes 4 servings*

Favorite recipe from *Wisconsin Milk Marketing Board*

TUSCAN PORK LOIN ROAST WITH FIG SAUCE

2 tablespoons olive oil
3 cloves garlic, minced
2 teaspoons coarse salt
2 teaspoons dried rosemary
½ teaspoon red pepper flakes *or* 1 teaspoon black pepper
1 center cut boneless pork loin roast (about 3 pounds)
¼ cup dry red wine
1 jar (about 8 ounces) dried fig spread

1. Preheat oven to 350°F. Combine oil, garlic, salt, rosemary and red pepper flakes in small bowl; brush over roast. Place pork on rack in shallow roasting pan.

2. Roast 1 hour or until internal temperature is 145°F. Transfer to cutting board. Tent with foil; let stand 10 minutes.

3. Meanwhile, pour wine into roasting pan; cook over medium-high heat 2 minutes, stirring to scrape up browned bits. Stir in fig spread; cook and stir until heated through. Cut pork into thin slices; serve with sauce.

Makes 6 to 8 servings

CLASSIC MEATBALL SOUP

- **1 egg**
- **4 tablespoons chopped fresh parsley, divided**
- **1 teaspoon salt, divided**
- **½ teaspoon dried marjoram leaves**
- **¼ teaspoon black pepper, divided**
- **½ cup soft fresh bread crumbs**
- **¼ cup grated Parmesan cheese**
- **1 pound ground beef**
- **3 cans (about 14 ounces each) beef broth**
- **3 stalks celery, cut into ¼-inch slices**
- **2 carrots, cut into ¼-inch slices**
- **1 can (about 14 ounces) whole peeled tomatoes, undrained**
- **½ cup uncooked rotini or small macaroni**
- **Salt and black pepper**

1. Preheat oven to 400°F. Grease 13×9-inch baking pan.

2. Combine egg, 3 tablespoons parsley, ½ teaspoon salt, marjoram and ⅛ teaspoon pepper in medium bowl; whisk lightly. Stir in bread crumbs and Parmesan. Add beef; mix well. Shape into 1-inch balls. Place meatballs in prepared pan.

3. Bake 20 to 25 minutes until meatballs are brown on all sides and cooked through, turning occasionally. Drain on paper towels..

4. Meanwhile, combine broth, celery and carrots in large saucepan or Dutch oven; bring to a boil over medium-high heat. Boil 10 minutes. Drain tomatoes, reserving juice. Chop tomatoes; add to broth with juice. Bring to a boil; boil 5 minutes.

5. Stir in pasta, remaining ½ teaspoon salt and ⅛ teaspoon pepper; cook 6 minutes, stirring occasionally. Add meatballs; cook 10 minutes over medium heat or until heated through. Stir in remaining 1 tablespoon parsley. Season with salt and pepper.

Makes 6 to 8 servings

SPINACH GNOCCHI

2 packages (10 ounces each) frozen chopped spinach
1 cup ricotta cheese
2 eggs
⅓ cup freshly grated Parmesan cheese
3 tablespoons all-purpose flour
½ teaspoon salt
⅛ teaspoon black pepper
⅛ teaspoon ground nutmeg
Marinara sauce
Shaved or grated Parmesan cheese

1. Cook spinach according to package directions. Drain well; let cool. Squeeze spinach dry; place in medium bowl. Stir in ricotta, eggs, grated Parmesan, flour, salt, pepper and nutmeg; mix well. Cover and refrigerate 1 hour.

2. Line baking sheet with parchment paper. Press heaping tablespoonful of spinach mixture between spoon and your hand to form oval gnocchi; place on prepared baking sheet. Repeat with remaining spinach mixture. Freeze gnocchi 30 minutes.

3. Bring large pot of salted water to a boil. Drop 8 to 12 gnocchi into boiling water; cook, uncovered, over medium heat about 2½ minutes or until gnocchi float to surface. Remove gnocchi with slotted spoon; drain on paper towels. Return water to a boil; repeat with remaining gnocchi.

4. Serve gnocchi with marinara sauce and shaved Parmesan cheese.

Makes 4 to 6 servings (about 32 gnocchi)

LEMON ROSEMARY ROASTED CHICKEN & POTATOES

4 bone-in chicken breast halves (with skin)
½ cup lemon juice
6 tablespoons olive oil, divided
6 cloves garlic, minced, divided
2 tablespoons plus 1 teaspoon chopped fresh rosemary leaves *or* 2¼ teaspoons dried rosemary
1½ teaspoons salt, divided
2 pounds small red potatoes, cut into quarters
1 large onion, cut into 2-inch chunks
¼ teaspoon black pepper

1. Place chicken in resealable food storage bag. Combine lemon juice, 3 tablespoons olive oil, 3 cloves minced garlic, 1 tablespoon rosemary and ½ teaspoon salt in small bowl; pour over chicken. Seal bag and gently shake until coated. Refrigerate several hours or overnight.

2. Preheat oven to 400°F. Place potatoes and onion in roasting pan. Combine remaining 3 tablespoons olive oil, 1 tablespoon rosemary, 3 cloves minced garlic, 1 teaspoon salt and pepper in small bowl; mix well. Pour over vegetables; stir to coat.

3. Remove chicken from bag; discard marinade. Arrange chicken in pan with vegetables; sprinkle with remaining 1 teaspoon rosemary.

4. Roast about 50 minutes or until chicken is cooked through (165°F) and potatoes are tender. Season with additional salt and pepper.

Makes 4 servings

VEGETABLE SPAGHETTI SAUCE WITH MEATBALLS

- **1 tablespoon olive oil**
- **1½ cups sliced fresh mushrooms**
- **½ cup plus 2 tablespoons finely chopped onion, divided**
- **½ cup chopped carrot**
- **½ cup chopped green bell pepper**
- **2 cloves garlic, minced**
- **2 cans (about 14 ounces each) stewed tomatoes, undrained**
- **1 can (6 ounces) tomato paste**
- **2½ teaspoons Italian seasoning, divided**
- **½ teaspoon salt**
- **¼ teaspoon black pepper**
- **1 egg white**
- **2 tablespoons fine dry bread crumbs**
- **8 ounces ground beef**
- **4 cups hot cooked spaghetti**

1. Preheat oven to 375°F. Heat oil in large saucepan over medium heat. Add mushrooms, ½ cup onion, carrot, bell pepper and garlic; cook and stir 4 to 5 minutes or until vegetables are crisp-tender. Stir in stewed tomatoes with juice, tomato paste, 2 teaspoons Italian seasoning, salt and black pepper. Bring to a boil over medium-high heat. Reduce heat to medium-low; cover and simmer 20 minutes, stirring occasionally.

2. Combine egg white, bread crumbs, remaining 2 tablespoons onion and ½ teaspoon Italian seasoning in medium bowl. Add beef; mix until well blended. Shape into 16 meatballs; place in 11×7-inch baking pan.

3. Bake 18 to 20 minutes or until meatballs are cooked through. Drain on paper towels.

4. Stir meatballs into sauce; return sauce to a boil. Reduce heat to medium-low; simmer, uncovered, about 10 minutes or until sauce thickens slightly, stirring occasionally. Serve over pasta.

Makes 4 servings

POTATO GNOCCHI WITH TOMATO SAUCE

- **2 pounds baking potatoes (3 or 4 large)**
- **Tomato Sauce (page 272) *or* 2 cups prepared meatless pasta sauce**
- **⅔ to 1 cup all-purpose flour, divided**
- **1 egg yolk**
- **½ teaspoon salt**
- **⅛ teaspoon ground nutmeg (optional)**
- **Grated Parmesan cheese**
- **Slivered fresh basil**

1. Preheat oven to 425°F. Pierce potatoes several times with fork. Bake 1 hour or until soft. Meanwhile, prepare Tomato Sauce.

2. Cut potatoes in half lengthwise; cool slightly. Scoop out potatoes from skins into medium bowl; discard skins. Mash potatoes until smooth. Add ⅓ cup flour, egg yolk, salt and nutmeg, if desired; mix well to form dough.

3. Turn out dough onto well-floured surface. Knead in enough remaining flour to form smooth dough. Divide dough into four pieces; roll each piece with hands on lightly floured surface into ¾- to 1-inch-wide rope. Cut each rope into 1-inch pieces; gently press thumb into center of each piece to make indentation. Transfer gnocchi to lightly floured kitchen towel in single layer to prevent sticking.

4. Bring 4 quarts salted water to a gentle boil in large saucepan or Dutch oven over high heat. To test cooking time, drop several gnocchi into water; cook 1 minute or until they float to surface. Remove from water with slotted spoon and taste for doneness. (If gnocchi start to dissolve, shorten cooking time by several seconds.) Cook remaining gnocchi in batches, removing with slotted spoon to warm serving dish.

5. Serve gnocchi with Tomato Sauce; sprinkle with Parmesan and basil.

Makes 4 servings

continued on page 272

Potato Gnocchi with Tomato Sauce, continued

TOMATO SAUCE

- **2 tablespoons olive oil or butter**
- **1 clove garlic, minced**
- **2 pounds ripe plum tomatoes, peeled, seeded and chopped**
- **1 teaspoon sugar**
- **¼ cup finely chopped prosciutto or cooked ham (optional)**
- **1 tablespoon finely chopped fresh basil**
- **Salt and black pepper**

Heat oil in medium saucepan over medium heat. Add garlic; cook 30 seconds or until fragrant. Stir in tomatoes and sugar; cook 10 minutes or until most of liquid has evaporated. Stir in prosciutto, if desired, and basil; cook 2 minutes. Season with salt and pepper. *Makes about 2 cups*

TUSCAN LAMB SKILLET

- **8 lamb rib chops (1½ pounds), cut 1 inch thick**
- **2 teaspoons olive oil**
- **3 teaspoons minced garlic**
- **1 can (19 ounces) cannellini beans, rinsed and drained**
- **1 can (about 14 ounces) Italian-style tomatoes, broken up, undrained**
- **1 tablespoon balsamic vinegar**
- **2 teaspoons minced fresh rosemary**

1. Trim fat from lamb chops. Heat oil in large skillet over medium heat. Add lamb; cook 8 minutes or until thermometer inserted into center registers 160°F for medium doneness, turning once. Transfer to large plate; keep warm.

2. Stir garlic into drippings in skillet; cook and stir 1 minute. Stir in beans, tomatoes with juice, vinegar and rosemary; bring to a boil. Reduce heat to medium-low; simmer 5 minutes.

3. Divide bean mixture among four plates; top with lamb chops.

Makes 4 servings

HOMEMADE SPINACH RAVIOLI

- 1 package (10 ounces) frozen chopped spinach, thawed and squeezed dry
- 1 cup ricotta cheese
- ½ cup grated Romano or Parmesan cheese
- 1 egg
- 1 tablespoon minced fresh basil
- ½ teaspoon salt
- ½ teaspoon black pepper
- ¼ teaspoon ground nutmeg
- 36 round wonton wrappers (thawed if frozen)
- 1 jar (about 26 ounces) marinara or other pasta sauce

1. Combine spinach, ricotta, Romano, egg, basil, salt, pepper and nutmeg in medium bowl; mix well. (Filling may be prepared up to 1 day in advance and refrigerated.)

2. Place two wonton wrappers on lightly floured surface, keeping remaining wrappers covered. Place 1 heaping teaspoon filling in center of each wrapper. Moisten edges around filling; top with second wrapper. Press edges gently around filling to remove air bubbles and seal. (If using square wrappers, cut out circles with 1½-inch round or scalloped cookie cutter, if desired.) Repeat with remaining wrappers and filling.

3. Bring large pot of salted water to a boil over high heat. Meanwhile, heat marinara sauce in medium saucepan over low heat. Add half of ravioli to boiling water; stir gently and cook over medium-high heat about 3 minutes or until ravioli float to surface. Remove ravioli to platter with with slotted spoon; keep warm. Repeat with remaining ravioli. Serve with marinara sauce.

Makes 18 ravioli (about 4 servings)

CHICKEN SCARPIELLO

3 tablespoons extra virgin olive oil, divided
1 pound spicy Italian sausage, cut into 1-inch pieces
1 (3-pound) chicken, cut into 10 pieces*
1 teaspoon salt, divided
1 large onion, chopped
2 red or orange bell peppers, cut into ¼-inch strips
3 cloves garlic, minced
½ cup dry white wine such as sauvignon blanc
½ cup chicken broth
½ cup coarsely chopped seeded hot cherry peppers
½ cup liquid from cherry pepper jar
1 teaspoon dried oregano
Additional salt and black pepper
¼ cup chopped fresh Italian parsley

**Or purchase 2 bone-in chicken leg quarters and 2 chicken breasts; separate drumsticks and thighs and cut breasts in half.*

1. Heat 1 tablespoon oil in large skillet over medium-high heat. Add sausage; cook about 10 minutes or until well browned on all sides, stirring occasionally. Remove sausage from skillet; set aside.

2. Heat 1 tablespoon oil in same skillet. Sprinkle chicken with ½ teaspoon salt; arrange skin side down in single layer in skillet (cook in batches if necessary). Cook about 6 minutes per side or until browned. Remove chicken from skillet; set aside. Drain oil from skillet.

3. Heat remaining 1 tablespoon oil in skillet. Add onion and remaining ½ teaspoon salt; cook and stir 2 minutes or until onion is softened, scraping up browned bits from bottom of skillet. Add bell peppers and garlic; cook and stir 5 minutes. Stir in wine; cook until liquid is reduced by half. Stir in broth, cherry peppers, cherry pepper liquid, oregano and additional salt and black pepper; bring to a simmer.

4. Return sausage and chicken along with any accumulated juices to skillet. Partially cover skillet and simmer 10 minutes. Uncover and simmer 15 minutes or until chicken is cooked through (165°F). Sprinkle with parsley.

Makes 4 to 6 servings

STUFFED PORK LOIN GENOA STYLE

1 (4- to 5-pound) boneless pork loin roast
1¼ cups fresh parsley sprigs, chopped and divided
½ cup fresh basil leaves, chopped
½ cup pine nuts
½ cup grated Parmesan cheese
6 cloves garlic, peeled and chopped
½ pound ground pork
½ pound Italian sausage
1 cup dry bread crumbs
¼ cup milk
1 egg
1 teaspoon ground black pepper

In food processor or blender, process 1 cup parsley, basil, pine nuts, Parmesan cheese and garlic. Set aside.

Mix together ground pork, Italian sausage, bread crumbs, milk, egg, remaining ¼ cup parsley and pepper.

Place roast fat side down on cutting board. Cut lengthwise down roast almost to, but not through, bottom; open like a book. Spread herb-cheese mixture over cut sides of roast; place ground pork mixture down center. Close halves; tie with kitchen string. Roast on rack in shallow baking pan at 350°F for 1½ hours or until internal temperature reaches 155°F. Slice to serve.

Makes 10 servings

Prep Time: 15 minutes **Cook Time:** 90 minutes

Favorite recipe from *National Pork Board*

The publisher would like to thank the companies and organizations listed below for the use of their recipes and photographs in this publication.

BelGioioso® Cheese Inc.

Campbell Soup Company

Cream of Wheat® Cereal

Del Monte Foods

Dole Food Company, Inc.

Filippo Berio® Olive Oil

Hormel Foods, LLC

Jennie-O Turkey Store, LLC

Kraft Foods Global, Inc.

National Pork Board

Reckitt Benckiser LLC.

Sonoma® Dried Tomatoes

StarKist®

Unilever

Wisconsin Milk Marketing Board

Index

Q

R

VOLUME MEASUREMENTS (dry)

1/8 teaspoon = 0.5 mL
1/4 teaspoon = 1 mL
1/2 teaspoon = 2 mL
3/4 teaspoon = 4 mL
1 teaspoon = 5 mL
1 tablespoon = 15 mL
2 tablespoons = 30 mL
1/4 cup = 60 mL
1/3 cup = 75 mL
1/2 cup = 125 mL
2/3 cup = 150 mL
3/4 cup = 175 mL
1 cup = 250 mL
2 cups = 1 pint = 500 mL
3 cups = 750 mL
4 cups = 1 quart = 1 L

VOLUME MEASUREMENTS (fluid)

1 fluid ounce (2 tablespoons) = 30 mL
4 fluid ounces (1/2 cup) = 125 mL
8 fluid ounces (1 cup) = 250 mL
12 fluid ounces (1 1/2 cups) = 375 mL
16 fluid ounces (2 cups) = 500 mL

WEIGHTS (mass)

1/2 ounce = 15 g
1 ounce = 30 g
3 ounces = 90 g
4 ounces = 120 g
8 ounces = 225 g
10 ounces = 285 g
12 ounces = 360 g
16 ounces = 1 pound = 450 g

DIMENSIONS

1/16 inch = 2 mm
1/8 inch = 3 mm
1/4 inch = 6 mm
1/2 inch = 1.5 cm
3/4 inch = 2 cm
1 inch = 2.5 cm

OVEN TEMPERATURES

250°F = 120°C
275°F = 140°C
300°F = 150°C
325°F = 160°C
350°F = 180°C
375°F = 190°C
400°F = 200°C
425°F = 220°C
450°F = 230°C

BAKING PAN SIZES

Utensil	Size in Inches/Quarts	Metric Volume	Size in Centimeters
Baking or Cake Pan (square or rectangular)	8×8×2	2 L	20×20×5
	9×9×2	2.5 L	23×23×5
	12×8×2	3 L	30×20×5
	13×9×2	3.5 L	33×23×5
Loaf Pan	8×4×3	1.5 L	20×10×7
	9×5×3	2 L	23×13×7
Round Layer Cake Pan	8×1½	1.2 L	20×4
	9×1½	1.5 L	23×4
Pie Plate	8×1¼	750 mL	20×3
	9×1¼	1 L	23×3
Baking Dish or Casserole	1 quart	1 L	—
	1½ quart	1.5 L	—
	2 quart	2 L	—